Cerinon Smith currently works as a trainer, consultant and clinician in the child care and protection. Many of the women she works with self-harm. Her published work includes two previous Women's Press Handbooks, *Living with Depression* co-authored with Kathy Nairn, and updated, with new material, *Protectors' Handbook: Reducing Abuse and Helping Children*

Dee Cox has an honours degree in Psychology from the Open University. She self-harmed for many years and was the driving force behind this book.

Jacqui Saradjian is a consultant clinical psychologist who is employed within the health service by Leeds Community Mental Health. She qualified as a clinical psychologist in 1992, and since then most of her therapeutic work has been with adults who have endured childhood trauma, and many of whom self-harm. Before this time, she worked as a teacher in residential settings, where she first cared for young women who self-harmed.

Also by Gerrilyn Smith from The Women's Press:

With Kathy Nairne *Dealing with Depression* (1984; and fully revised and updated, with new material, 1995)
The Protectors' Handbook: Reducing the Risk of Child Abuse and Helping Children Recover (1995)

GERRILYN SMITH, DEE COX AND JACQUI SARADJIAN

Women and and Self-Harm

First published by The Women's Press Ltd, 1998
A member of the Namara Group
34 Great Sutton Street, London EC1V 0DX

British Library Cataloguing-in-Publication Data
A catalogue record for this book is available from the British Library.

ISBN 0 7043 4440 8

Typeset in 11/12pt Sabon by FSH Ltd, London
Printed and bound in Great Britain by Cox & Wyman Ltd,
Reading, Berkshire

To my mother, Barbara, who taught me to love myself
and Annmarie, who struggles so hard to do so.
Gerrilyn

To Steve, for being so patient.
Dee

To Lindsey, to give voice to your suffering.
Jacqui

Contents

Foreword   1

Chapter 1: What is Self-Harm and Who Does It?   6
Chapter 2: Explanations of Self-Harm   26
Chapter 3: Getting Access to Services   45
Chapter 4: Conventional Treatments   57
Chapter 5: Self-Help   77
Chapter 6: Disrupting Self-Harm Patterns   90
Chapter 7: Family and Friends   111

Afterword   128
Notes   137
Appendix I: Drugs Commonly Prescribed to
              Women Who Self-Harm   143
Appendix II: Further Reading   147
Appendix III: Resources   151

Foreword

This book needed to be written a long time ago. Self-harm, deliberate injury to the body, is nothing new. People have self-harmed over time and across cultures; often in secret and often in shame. It is only recently that self-harm has been recognised as a serious problem that many people suffer with all of their lives, often despairing in their isolation because of the great veil of secrecy which still surrounds the subject. We have written this book with the hope of breaking down some of that secrecy and also of reducing some of the isolation that those of us who self-harm often feel.

We ourselves have each had experience of self-harm; both personally and professionally. For years Dee used self-harm as a way of coping with difficult and distressing feelings. She has also run a self-help telephone line for others struggling in similar ways. Both Jacqui and Gerrilyn are Clinical Psychologists and their professional activies involve working with women who self-harm. In addition both Jacqui and Gerrilyn have each fostered daughters whose self-harming behaviour led to numerous casualty visits, multiple admissions for inpatient treatment, the prescribing of psychotropic medication, and various forms of therapy. These young women have received a tremendous amount of help, both good and bad over the years, much of which they took unquestioningly in their desperation for an end to their suffering. For Jacqui and Gerrilyn as foster parents and primary care givers, help was completely lacking. Both have known the pain and anguish of watching someone they love repeatedly hurting themselves and at times appearing as if they were slowly dying before their very eyes.

Writing this book comes out of the distress and at times despair that all three of us have witnessed and experienced through self-harming behaviours. Our collaboration began when Dee recognised the need for a self-help book on self-harm and decided to approach The Women's Press. Her choice of publisher reflects the fact that self-harm, in the main, is a female phenomenon. This is not to say that men do not self-harm. Self-harming behaviour is most often connected to early traumatic experiences for which there was a lack of appropriate care-giving. The trauma and the associated emotions could not be effectively dealt with at that time and so the individual retained a high level of residual anger and pain. Those feelings must be expressed and addressed but sometimes that can seem an impossible task. Primarily self-harm is a way of dealing with such feelings when they become too difficult to acknowledge and manage.

In our culture women are often taught how to manage other people's feelings at the expense of managing their own, whereas men are taught to manage their own at the expense of others. In particular being angry has often been deemed 'unfeminine' and yet one of the most powerful emotional responses to trauma is anger. Anger can be a reasonable response to unreasonable events. Learning how to manage angry feelings is an important developmental task for us all. Anger in little boys is condoned. They are usually encouraged to express their anger and even be aggressive and fight back. They are often taught to channel their aggression through competition and 'tough' sporting activity. Maybe times are changing and the same message is also being given to girls. But for those of us who grew up without the wider influence of feminism encouraging our parents to allow us to develop all of our selves, there were (and probably still are) strong prohibitions against expressing strong emotions. Instead we were taught that females should be nurturing, caring, and protecting of others. In a distorted way to injure oneself could be seen as morally superior to injuring others, no matter how injurious those others may have been towards us; by directing anger inwards towards ourselves, we successfully protect others from the full fury of our anger. It seems to us that this is what tips the balance in the gender ratio.

In the main, this book addresses women who self-harm. We have tried to write the book so that the voices of these women can really be heard above the din of the psychiatric labelling and hostility they often meet. Ironically, these reactions often come from the very professionals who are supposed to be offering them care. Unfortunately these negative responses can also sometimes come from those who are supposed to love them, such as family and friends. The hurt that is inflicted on women by professionals or those close to them is sometimes intentional, sometimes unintentional; and is most often inflicted through ignorance, fear and distress. Therefore this book also aims to include those who care for and support a person who self-harms, either personally or professionally, so that some of this ignorance, fear and distress can be reduced. In doing so we hope to promote a co-operative approach to recovery.

In this book what we are describing is the sense we

have made from our personal and professional experiences of self-harm; who does it; and the explanations used to try and explain it. We then review the various forms of help available – the psychiatric and psychological treatments that are provided – and examine women's experience of those treatments, both good and bad. In doing this we hope to provide women with a more informed choice of what is available. We also look at the impact of self-harm on others and conclude with some suggested ways of interrupting self-harm patterns, which the women we have come to know have found useful. At the end of the book there is a reference list and resources for those who want to know more.

Throughout the book we have used personal testimonies from women who self-harm. These are used with their permission. Many were sent to Dee by women in response to articles or publicity related to her work with the help-line. After every event, letters would come in. Having had the courage to speak and write publicly about her own experience of self-harm, Dee made it possible for others to write and acknowledge their secret. In their testimonies, many themes emerge; thoughts, feelings and actions carried out in pain and privacy. We hope that all our readers can draw strength from both the similarities and the differences in experience.

When viewed in the context of a woman's life experience, self-harm makes sense. Of course, this does not mean we encourage women to self-harm, nor do we disregard the seriousness of the effects of self-harming behaviour. We recognise that left unresolved self-harm can have devastating consequences. But we believe that the more knowledge and understanding women who self-harm and those who care for them can gain, the more likely it is that they can begin to find ways of interrupting this pattern of behaviour. So we hope that this book gives you, the reader, whoever you may be, a better understanding of self-harm and guides you to people and resources that are committed to ending the inner pain.

Gerrilyn Smith, Dee Cox and Jacqui Saradjian

Chapter 1
What is Self-Harm and
Who Does it?

What is Self-Harm?

Feeling dissatisfied with yourself, how you look, the person you are, or how you feel is an almost universal female experience within our culture. Even when we outwardly reject the cultural mores, many of us are still left with internalised feelings of inadequacy, of not quite 'measuring up'. Women, in particular, are encouraged to focus on their appearance and body shape – hence the success of special diets, low-fat foods, slimming aids and cosmetic surgery. With such negative messages surrounding us, it is not surprising that many women damage or try to alter their bodies in a number of ways. These can include socially acceptable, and even encouraged, practices such as hair-plucking, cosmetic surgery, body-piercing, and skin-bronzing; socially tolerated behaviour such as smoking, regular over-consumption of alcohol, and dangerous sports; and self-destructive behaviour such as eating disorders, alcohol and drug abuse, sexual risk-taking, and elective surgery.[1]

Although all of the above cause injury to the body in some form or other, they are not the same as deliberate self-harm. The connection between the action and the injury is distant in both time and intent, and most of us would not think of practices such as hair-plucking or piercing as self-harm at all. Other behaviour such as smoking causes harm to the body in the long term but the immediate intent is not to damage oneself.

This book is written primarily for those women who, by a variety of methods, cause more direct and immediate injury to their bodies, and clearly intend to do so. When the term *self-harm* is used, we are referring specifically to behaviour which produces immediate, unambiguous injury. This type of behaviour has been given many names by professionals such as self-mutilation, self-injury, self-attack, para-suicide, deliberate non-fatal act, and symbolic wounding. We have decided to use self-harm because we feel that that is more descriptive and less judgemental than many of the other terms used.

So what actually constitutes self-harm? Women who self-harm have described a large number of ways in which they have caused injury to their bodies including:

- Cutting
- Stabbing
- Scratching the skin
- Scraping/Rubbing their skin, removing the top layer to make a sore
- Placement of sharp objects under the skin or in body orifices
- Gnawing at flesh
- Biting the inside of the mouth making sores and regularly re-opening them
- Picking at wounds
- Burning skin by physical means using heat
- Burning skin by chemical means using caustic liquids

- Pulling hair out – including eyelashes, eyebrows
- Hitting themselves hard enough to cause bruises or break bones
- Banging the head against something
- Tying ligatures around the neck, arms or legs to restrict the flow of blood
- Ingesting small amounts of toxic substances or objects to cause discomfort and damage but with no intention to die

Of course, many of these will cause a visible wound to the body but women have been made to feel so guilty and ashamed of the injuries, and/or have experienced other inappropriate responses, that they tend to hide their cuts, bruises and scars. If anyone does notice, the injuries are frequently passed off as accidents. People tend to accept this, often unlikely, explanation as it is easier to do so than to recognise the reality of the pain the woman must feel in order to hurt herself in such a way.

This guilt and shame resulting in the need to hide the behaviour can begin at a very young age. When she was about seven years old, Dee witnessed an horrific accident which culminated in the death of her best friend. Those with whom she should have been able to talk, and get care and comfort from, were unavailable to her. They had decided it was 'best' if the traumatic event was not talked about. Consequently Dee was left with a myriad of painful feelings that she was unable to deal with:

My parents and the school decided that it was best if it wasn't mentioned again but I didn't feel the same way as they did. It was such a harrowing experience and I felt so bad that I began to hurt myself to take away my bad feelings. This self-harm consisted of scraped knees or picked scabs which meant I could visit the school nurse for cuddles. I also tried cutting my hands with scissors which seemed pretty effective but I had to explain away the cuts which I did by blaming the dog.

As Dee got older she began cutting her arms and like so many women who do so, hid the cuts and scars under long-sleeved clothing. Some women describe the pressure of feelings that lead them to self-harm to be so intense that they 'just do it without thinking exactly where'. Other women describe deliberately choosing to self-harm only the parts of their bodies that can easily be covered up. Patricia was physically, sexually and emotionally abused as a child and started self-harming from an early age. She continued to hurt herself into adulthood. Her mother was dependent on alcohol and could not give Patricia the emotional support and care she needed. She says:

> I hurt my skin where it could not be seen and felt as though I'd beaten the abusers by destroying my body before they could...I applied for a nursing course...I found the training very stressful and although I loved my job, I began to cut myself on the stomach and legs with razor blades and glass. At times my body was criss-crossed with superficial cuts from chest to knees and it resembled a piece of meat. I put on my uniform and no one had any idea.

In 1989, a study was published of 240 women who self-harmed.[2] One of the areas they looked at was where the women chose to inflict their injuries. The women interviewed indicated that they attacked certain parts of their bodies more often then others. They reported damage to:

- their arms (particularly the wrists)   74 per cent
- their legs   44 per cent
- their abdomens   25 per cent
- their heads   23 per cent

- their chests (the study did not differentiate
  between chest and breasts)   18 per cent
- their genitals   8 per cent

Most research on self-harm has shown a similar general pattern.[3] However, we have found that a greater proportion of the women who talked to us have attacked parts of their bodies specifically connected to their female identity such as faces, breasts and genitals. This could reflect our shared gender, as women working with women are more likely to disclose this type of information. Some women particularly target these parts of their bodies as they have been sexually abused and have learnt to hate the parts of their bodies connected with the experience. It is also a way of communicating the physical pain that they have felt.

He used to say how lovely my breasts were. Pert he called them. Said they were like pure marble. He said my nipples would stand out showing how much I wanted him, but I didn't, I never did. Well they are not lovely now. My breasts are a mass of scars... sometimes I cut inside my vagina too. That's how he made me feel, as if I was being cut apart inside.

Lucy

I was babysitting and saw some tablets in a cupboard. I took about 12 of them without knowing what they were. I just wanted to hurt my insides... That is probably when I thought about destroying my insides, even though the abuse had stopped. I became obsessed with destroying my insides because they were contaminated by HIM.

Ellen

The vast majority of women who self-harm tend to do so repeatedly, although single episodes of self-harming behaviour are unlikely to show up in statistics unless the injury has been so bad it requires hospital treatment. Most women also describe using more than one method to inflict harm on their bodies. The method they choose can depend on various factors including what is available at the time. Some women say that the way they harm themselves depends on what sort of feelings trigger the need to self-harm in the first place. Christine has described the number of ways in which she self-harms.

> I've tried most sorts of self-harm the most frequent being cutting or stabbing...I smash bottles and on one occasion smashed a glass panel, but normally I use a scalpel or razor blades (all numbered and used in sequence until they are blunt)...I also burn myself... with an iron or with boiling water or with cotton wool soaked in chemicals strapped to my hands. Blisters are pulled off and scabs are cut open...I also bruise myself, hitting myself with anything that is available.
>
> Christine

> Talking about it over and over in therapy, I realised that I do it in different ways at different times. When I'm filled with feelings connected to him, I tend to cut myself. When I am angry, really angry and frustrated I'm more likely to hit myself, bruise myself. When I feel cut off, blank, as if I'm both alive and dead at the same time, it's then that I tend to burn myself. It is as if I haven't the energy to hurt myself in a more active way.
>
> Lucy

Virtually all women who self-harm tend to do so when alone. Some women say that this is because they believe that what they do separates them 'from the rest of humankind and [they] let no one or almost no one know about an act that they regard as shameful'.[4] This shame is often caused by other people being too ready to condemn, rather than trying to understand women who harm themselves. Some women may self-harm alone because they feel that this is something entirely personal, a need only they know about and only they can deal with. Like so many women, they cope with their own feelings privately in the only way they know how, developing an apparently tough outer shell and driving the pain, the anger and hurt deep inside. Patricia experienced this split between her internal reality and the 'happy face' she put on for others:

I began to add to my emotional shell and on the outside seemed loud and confident, but inside the pain and anger were slowly building up. I began to scald myself when I was on my own, which was a comfort.

Patricia

On rare occasions, and usually in specific circumstances, women self-harm together. An example of such circumstances is when young women have been placed together in institutions. This has often led to professionals construing self-harming behaviour as a 'copy cat' phenomena. However in such environments, these women describe feeling increased powerlessness, invalidation and disqualification – all feelings associated with self-injurious behaviour. It is not surprising therefore when, isolated from society in similar ways and experiencing similar feelings, women find solace in doing the same thing together. It is not, however, solely within institutions that young women can seek this type of comfort. Dee coped with not being allowed to talk about her extremely painful feelings by self-harming, and felt drawn to a friend who seemed to be experiencing a similar problem.

My new friend was sitting on a windowsill cutting her arm with a razor blade. It intrigued me so I tried it too and found it therapeutic: it released the tension I was feeling at the time. We soon became very close friends indeed, spending many nights listening to morbid music and writing morbid poetry and cutting up...Other school friends were very sarcastic and decided that we were probably suicidal, which of course we weren't.

Dee

Self-harm and Suicide

There is a mistaken belief that self-harm is the same as attempted suicide. However although self-harm causes direct injury to the body, usually these wounds are not directly life-threatening. These are not futile suicide gestures – the intention is to harm, not to kill. Only a very small percentage of people who self-harm have been found to commit suicide in later years.[5] So self-harming behaviour *in itself* is rarely evidence of suicidal intent. On the contrary, many women who self-harm say that they do so in order to make it possible *to live*; to relieve the painful states of consciousness they feel so that they can cope with other aspects of living. In fact, at times a woman may feel so bad that self-harm can be a way of averting a suicide attempt.

Self-injury continues the discourse of a person's life, whereas a suicide attempt separates a person from that discourse, removing the individual from their awareness and from being.[6]

However, sometimes the emotional distress a woman feels can become so unbearable that self-harm does not seem able to relieve the tension and a suicide attempt feels like the only escape.

The mental pain torments me constantly,
no matter how deep I cut, cutting no longer eases the pain
I want this pain to stop.

People are convinced that in time things will change
but they are outside looking in,
I'm on the inside feeling it all
I want to fade away, to not be here at all.

Tyler

At such times women often say that they find themselves
in the dreadful conflict of knowing that they should and
need to talk to someone about these thoughts and
feelings yet feel they do not have the words nor the
emotional ability to be able to communicate the intensity
of their despair and distress. When you feel like this it is
very hard to approach others; you may doubt that they
will be able to hear what you are saying or be able to
share the level of distress you are feeling. But it is
precisely at these times that it is really important you
should find someone. Help-lines can be a good source of
support in such times of crisis.

Who Self-Harms?

There is no one particular 'kind' of woman who self-
harms, nor is self-harming behaviour restricted to any
particular race. Women who self-harm range from young
to old; rich to poor; fat to thin; single to those with a
partner; educated to uneducated; in a successful profes-
sion to being unemployed. But because the factors which
contribute to the desire to self-harm are more likely to
arise in certain circumstances, some patterns do emerge.

Because so much self-harm is carried out in secrecy, it
is extremely difficult to gain any real picture of the actual
number of people who have, at some time in their lives,
caused deliberate harm to their body. A report from the
first conference in Britain on self-harm stated that
100,000 individuals seek help from the health services
each year. This will, of course, be an underestimate as it

counts only those who have actually gone for help.

Almost all the information that is available has come from hospital accident and emergency departments. In one study it was estimated that at least 1 in 600 people self-harm to such an extent that they need hospital treatment.[7] The authors of the study recognise '*this is likely to be an underestimate since some deliberate self-harm will be concealed by relatives, friends or the person themselves, or will not be judged sufficiently severe to require hospital assessment*' (p.453). The same study found that twice as many people who went to accident and emergency departments had self-poisoned compared to those who self-wounded. This is not surprising as many women have told us that they rarely go to accident and emergency departments when they have self-harmed but are more likely to do so if they have poisoned themselves. This is reflected in the findings of another study which noted that at least 80 per cent of patients who went to a hospital for self-poisoning had also recently self-wounded and had not sought treatment for those injuries.[8]

Gender

As we have already seen, socialisation leads to different expectations of men and women. Considering these differential expectations of our society helps us understand why women are much more likely than men to deliberately self-harm. Women in general are expected to hold less power than men and there are different expectations as to the tasks we will perform and the positions we will subsequently hold. Women tend to be offered less opportunities in life and are generally treated with less respect than men. We tend to receive less reward, tangible and intangible, for the work we do and the roles we play; we are often made to feel less important and our opinions less valid. Women are encouraged to compromise rather than question; to acquiesce rather than agitate.

Importantly, society's construction of the male does not automatically include the idea that men should be nurturing and caring, but it does assume the notion that men's needs should and will be catered for, and that men should actively express their feelings of anger and aggression. Women, on the other hand, are expected to meet the needs of others, often at personal expense. We are to tolerate passively situations in which we feel used, abused and powerless. The predictable consequence is feelings of worthlessness, anger and frustration, yet we are so rarely encouraged to voice these emotions, that we often take them back into ourselves. As the author and poet, Adrienne Rich writes: '*Most women have not even begun to touch this anger except to drive it inward like a rusty nail.*'

My eyes burn with hatred and rage,
I glare at everyone around me, not meaning to
but I can't stop it – the hatred is so strong inside me.
I'm scared of it getting out, frightened that it will be
    expressed as violence.
I scream inside
wanting so much to scream out loud
but I am unable to show so much anger, so much pain,
so the screams swirl around my head
driving me over the edge
towards something self-destructive.

Tyler

Interestingly when men feel unable, for whatever reason, to exert power over their own lives, when they are put into situations which force them to be passive, some men begin to self-harm. This is particularly evident in places such as prisons, when some men who have never previously self-harmed begin to do so. As society changes and men gradually lose their privileged status, it is likely that the rates of self-harm for men will increase.

This pattern of change is already evident in the dramatic increase in the rate of eating disorders for men. Male anorexia is something that is researched and recognised. The focus on male body image is increasing, a fact highlighted by the booming market for men's health magazines and articles on body shape and tone. There is also more emphasis placed on personal grooming for men and with that, pressure for men to conform to new stereotypes of male appearance and behaviour.[9]

Some studies do show equal numbers of males that self-harm to females. Perhaps this is because the statistics are collected from accident and emergency departments and men are more likely to go for treatment for their injuries than women. Research on male suicide shows a similar pattern. Statistics indicate that more men commit suicide than women but this masks the fact that more women actually attempt suicide. The difference arises from the fact that when men try to harm or kill themselves, they tend to use more violent methods and consequently are more likely to succeed.

Race

It is a lamentable fact that black women still suffer racial prejudice in this country. Racism and the resulting bullying and harassment, potentially increases the isolation and stress suffered by black women. In addition, as women they experience the effects of living in a sexist society. Institutionalised racism can lead to negative feelings about some aspects of black identity such as skin colour, hair texture and the shape of facial features.[10] This in turn can lead to attacks on these aspects of self deemed as indicative of 'blackness'. These 'attacks' are often sanctioned by the wider dominant white culture. This social pressure may be especially powerful in the case of young black women raised separately from their families of origin and placed trans-racially in either adoptive/foster families, or residential care.[11]

It is also true that many families and communities help to build up a child's self-esteem, stressing pride in their colour and heritage. This can help inoculate the child against the stresses and invalidation that racism perpetuates.

In terms of actual research, there has been little investigation into the incidence of self-harming behaviour in any racial group other than Caucasian and more needs to be carried out. Arnold From their own work, and that of colleagues, Gloria Babiker and Lois Arnold, have found a relatively high incidence of self-harming behaviour among young Asian and Black women living in Britain. Given the connection between invalidating environments and self-harming behaviour, it should not be surprising that Black, Asian and other women from minority ethnic groups will show high levels of self-harming behaviour. Babiker and Arnold suggest that the women's struggle to deal with the pressure of living within conflicting cultures – that of their family of origin and community *and the wider dominant white community* – also adds to the stress these women might feel. They also describe how women have made direct connections between experiences of racism and their subsequent self-harm.

Age

From all that is written about women who self-harm, it would seem that the most typical age that this begins is at the younger end of the adult age range; between 16 to 25 years of age (60 per cent).[12] One reason for this might be that the type of injury caused at this stage is more 'recognisable' as self-harm. It could also be a reflection of the fact that with the onset of puberty, many of us become more aware of the pressures, restrictions and demands on us as women. However, there is no absolute rule – women reported beginning to self-harm at all ages; the youngest age of onset was 6 years and the oldest was 75 years.

Statistics would suggest that older women are less likely to self-harm than younger women. This may be because as women get older they tend to have less demands and pressures on them – social, personal and sexual – and they may have learnt alternative coping strategies. Another contributing factor is that older women may be less likely to seek help, in part because the help they have received in the past has been so inadequate and in some cases demeaning.

Many people do not recognise that young children can also self-harm yet many adults describe beginning to self-harm at an early age. Several adult women have told us that from a relatively young age they engaged in acts of deliberate self-harm which were not recognised as such, sometimes not even by the woman themselves. They described harming themselves in different ways at different ages; one kind of self-harming behaviour being replaced by another. This substitution is not unusual – for example it is reported that 10–15 per cent of children engage in head-banging behaviour. That percentage decreases as children get older but they may just be substituting different behaviour that is not so blatant.

My older sister remembers the tantrums I had when I was a toddler. My mother took me to the GP just before I started school because they were so bad. I would scream and bang my head over and over on the floor. I've cut my head open several times. I always had cuts and bruises and I'd never leave my cuts alone. I'd pick and pick at the scabs and make them bleed. I don't remember exactly when, but once when I didn't have a scab to pick, I bit my knuckle on my finger and made myself bleed. For years I was always in trouble for picking my scars. I don't remember a time when I did not have scars. I was always falling over and cutting myself but the wounds would never heal as I would pick at them. When I was almost eight years old, I 'fell' over a cliff. I knew what I was doing, I walked further to the edge and then there was no more ground and I was falling. Soon after that I took my first overdose.

Debbie

Research from Oxford reflects the fact that women can and do begin to self-harm when they are very young – 5.3 per cent of all patients referred to a large general hospital for self-harming behaviour were under 16 years of age and more than 1 in 5 of these had self-harmed before.[13]

People with Disabilities

A large number of people who have learning disabilities and other forms of disability self-harm, many of whom will never be able to tell us in words what it is they are feeling, nor what has happened to cause them such distress. However, even if a woman has a disability that prevents her from speaking, she can usually communicate in other ways to people who are motivated enough to try and understand.

Often self-harming behaviour is noted in institutional or communal facilities. The explanations given in the professional literature have been various but most relate to the need of the person to stimulate themselves or to gain the attention of carers. Over the past few years, however, the emotional deprivation and neglect that people with disabilities have suffered in such institutions has begun to be recognised, as has the very large percentage who have been sexually and physically abused. In addition whether or not they are in institutions, people with disabilities are very often excluded from society. They are often made to feel flawed and somehow less than human. They are treated as if they have few if any 'normal feelings' which leads to feelings of rejection, alienation, silencing and exclusion. These are the same feelings described by other women who self-harm.

It is important to note here that although many disabled people do self-harm as a result of their emotional distress, they are also very vulnerable to being physically abused. The perpetrator of that abuse may explain away the injuries he or she has inflicted as self-harm, an explanation that is too often accepted without question.

Trauma in the Lives of Those who Self-Harm

We have seen that the circumstances of our lives as women have a profound impact on how we feel about ourselves, yet in many ways women who self-harm are significant for the differences in their circumstances rather than the similarities. Nevertheless there is a common factor in the lives of all women who self-harm. When talking about themselves and their experiences, they tell us that during their childhood years they have experienced trauma; physical abuse, sexual abuse, severe emotional abuse, repeated surgery and/or invasive medical treatment; and other forms of trauma such as witnessing violence.[14] Many professionals still fail to make this link, while others state the connection very clearly.

When a client routinely self-mutilates, we know for certain that this woman has been badly intruded on in childhood. What we do not know is how.[15]

Not everyone who has experienced childhood trauma responds by self-harming. What seems to affect whether or not we do, is whether or not the emotional care we received after that traumatic experience was appropriate. We are all taught, to a lesser or greater extent, to recognise and cope with our emotions by those who care for us when we are very young. A child learns to recognise and to reduce emotional arousal by her parent or carer noticing the child's emotional state, attending to the child, and accurately reflecting, mirroring and verbally interpreting that emotion for the child. It is as if for a brief period of time that emotion is jointly held between the child and the adult. As the carer reduces his or her emotional state, the child follows, this time mirroring the carer. As the child is comforted by her carer, over time, she learns to identify her emotions, reduce her emotional arousal and at times of great emotional distress when she feels she cannot deal with her own emotional state, she learns to seek care and comfort from another person. The carer does not even have to get it right every time. The child can cope well with good-enough care.

A trauma is an inescapable stressful event or series of events which overwhelm a person's existing coping mechanisms. Consequently, traumatic experiences give rise to emotional turmoil. If appropriate help and care are not given to children to help them cope with those feelings, they have to find their own solution; to cope the best way they can. Children find many ways to do this and some children do so by engaging in various acts such as sucking, biting, eating, temper tantrums, aggression to others, rocking, head-banging, all of which bring about calm feelings. This can help us cope but we do not learn about a) relying on other people for care-giving and comfort and b) how to cope any other way with distressing emotional states.

It also seems that the younger a child is when the

trauma occurs for which she did not get the care she needed, the more likely she is to engage in self-harming behaviour; *'behaviour patterns originating in painful encounters...in the first years of life'*.[16] When we are young we develop patterns which help us cope and which quite often remain with us for the rest of our lives. It is during the first few years of our lives that we learn about being cared for and having our needs met but for some of us this can be when we first experience neglect and feelings of worthlessness. Women who self-harm are much more likely to have grown up in families where, generally, their emotional needs were not met, or where they were neglected or repeatedly separated from those who did care for them.[17] Some women may have had families who seemed to care very well for them; providing for them materially and practically but at the same time not recognising, or providing for, their emotional needs. Other families may have responded inappropriately, even though they were doing so out of the 'best' of intentions.

It was a Saturday afternoon. I can see it in my head, like a video, the memory is that clear even though I was only four years old. I was playing with my cousin in our front garden. We saw the men come out of the pub. My dad came out because of the noise and went to try and break up the fight. They turned on him and stabbed him, over and over again. I ran screaming daddy daddy daddy. I tried to get him up, I didn't know he was dead. I was covered in his blood and cut by the glass, my blood mixed with his. We never talked about it. The doctor told my mum I'd forget it sooner that way.

Steph

Gloria Babiker and Lois Arnold have suggested that for women who start self-harming in childhood or adolescence the causes must lie in their early years. They go on to say that those who begin to self-harm in adulthood often have also had negative childhood experiences, but the self-harm may have been triggered by a significant event in the woman's adult life. The emotions arising from the original trauma have not been processed so they remain stored, as if in a capsule, along with all the events that were connected to it such as sights, smells, sensations, noises. Even though they appear to be pushed away and cut off from consciousness, any similar sights, smells, sensations, and noises can become reminders of, or triggers to, the trauma which can evoke intrusive images; a repeated replaying of distressing memories. Sometimes the memory of the actual event does not come to mind (and paradoxically we may not remember much of what happened), but there can be overwhelmingly powerful emotions or bodily feelings that seem to be totally unrelated to what is currently happening in our everyday lives. Triggers to the memory of the trauma may become increasingly more subtle and generalised and things that appear irrelevant can become reminders of the trauma. *'The personal meaning of the traumatic experience evolves over time and often includes feelings of irretrievable loss, anger, betrayal and helplessness...one particular event can activate other long-forgotten memories of a previous trauma'.*[18]

The events women most commonly described that trigger these states, are feelings or images directly related to a traumatic experience; or difficulties in relationships; particularly if those difficulties involve feelings of rejection, separations or abandonment.

It would seem that the most common events that lead to self-harm beginning in adulthood are rape and serious physical assaults – most often by a partner. Other adult women begin self-harming after the loss or death of someone close to them such as a partner, parent or child.

> I began to cut myself soon after my mother died. It was then I seemed to suddenly realise that I had never really had a mother, she had never wanted me nor cared about me. It had always been like that. I had had no one.
>
> Sarah

When we are experiencing high levels of distress, it is vital for our well-being that we are able to communicate these feelings. But if these emotional signals are not heard and recognised, then we cannot obtain the care we need to comfort us and alleviate that intense pain. It is likely that women who self-harm have had to endure overwhelming levels of emotional distress, at some time in their lives, most probably during their formative years. Human beings are unable to tolerate such high levels of distress and this produces an urgent need to find a way to reduce those feelings and an alternative means of communicating with others the nature of the feelings that are generating so much anguish. Harming oneself can become the response to such overwhelming experiences. It can produce a physiological change within the body biochemistry itself bringing about a sense of calm. The scars it leaves are visible evidence of the pain endured; a message to the outside world.

Whether you are someone who self-harms or you are reading this book because you care about someone who does and want to help them, the first step in the process is to recognise that the you are not alone, if you self-harm you are not that unusual nor are you that different from other people.

Chapter 2
Explanations of Self-Harm

Many women are desperate to stop self-harming but are too wary to seek help. Women have told us that in part this wariness is based on a fear that they will not be understood and that their self-harm will be interpreted in a way that bears little or no resemblance to their own personal experience. They say that the interpretations that many professionals over the years have put on their behaviour often minimises what they consider to be most important and maximises what they consider to be least important. Some say that they also worry that if they try to get help, they will be given a psychiatric label with all the stigma that entails. Additionally, women have told us that they have also had some negative experiences of counselling and therapy as again the particular therapists they saw had their own under-standing of self-harm which they wanted to impose on the woman's experience.

However, if you self-harm, it is important to remember that there are also some very good psychiatrists, and good therapists and counsellors who will be able to help you make sense of your own experience and in doing so work with you on the issues which surface, which can eventually lead you to stop self-harming. Being able to make sense of your own experience of self-harm and being aware of the labels that are likely to be used in the professional psychiatric context is an important skill. Therefore we have written this chapter which looks at the models professionals use to interpret self-harming. These may or may not fit with your own understanding. These explanations may be useful in elaborating or revising what you have previously thought about self-harm, or they may not fit at all, but they will equip you with the information you need to make your own decision. It is important that you and those who support you, consider a wide range of possible explanations. You should not feel you have to settle for an explanation solely on the basis of a professional opinion, especially if it doesn't feel right for you.

We describe both typical psychiatric and psychological explanations as to why some women self-harm. Psychiatric explanations tend to see self-harm as a symptom of some form of diagnosable mental illness due to physiological disturbances in the brain or an 'untreatable' personality disorder. Consequently psychiatrists, who are trained medical doctors, are more likely to treat self-harm by using drugs or other physical treatments. Psychological explanations tend to look at the thoughts and feelings that lead a person to self-harm, and what has happened in that person's life to give rise to those emotions. They also look at the various functions self-harm performs within the context of the woman's life. Consequently, psychologists and psycho-therapists, trained to help people make changes to their behaviour, are likely to use treatments which help a woman to find the origins and functions of her self-harm, to express the feelings that lead to self-harm, and to find other ways of coping with these emotions.

In reality many psychiatrists now see that there is a psychological dimension to self-harm, and many psychologists recognise that there are also physiological changes which take place when a person consistently causes injury to their own body.

We describe psychiatric explanations first as these are often the first interpretations women encounter when meeting professionals.

Self-Harm as a Symptom of Psychiatric Disorder

When women who self-harm come into contact with the psychiatric services, they tend to be labelled as 'ill'. Self-harming behaviour can be seen as 'deviant' (bad) and 'histrionic' (attention-seeking) or evidence of a specific psychiatric illness; it is classified as a fault in the workings of the brain.

Personality Disorders

Various diagnoses are given, the most likely being that of **Personality Disorder**. A diagnosis of personality disorder is given when a person's behaviours, beliefs and attitudes are deemed to be inflexible and maladaptive to such an extent that it causes that person significant difficulties in social and occupational contexts or causes that person serious distress.[1] There are various types of personality disorder depending on the kind of 'maladaptive characteristics' that the person is judged to have.

Women who self-harm are most frequently given a diagnosis of **borderline personality disorder (BPD)**. People diagnosed as BPD are seen as individuals who have unstable relationships, erratic emotions, poor self-image, and who engage in impulsive acts such as eating sprees, stealing, gambling, sex, and/or self-harming behaviour.

The second most common diagnosis is of *histrionic personality disorder*, the characteristics of which are judged to be interpersonal problems, being overly dramatic and attention-seeking, dependent and constantly demanding.

Judith Herman, herself a psychiatrist, describes giving a woman a diagnosis of a personality disorder as *'little more than a sophisticated insult'*.[2] Women given such diagnoses are often treated by professionals with overt hostility. As there is no medication that can be given to change 'the personality', anyone with such a diagnosis is deemed by psychiatrists to be intrinsically 'untreatable'. This of course frustrates some psychiatrists who work mainly by prescribing drugs or other forms of physical treatment. Thus they can project their frustration on to the patient. They may prescribe drugs for some of the symptoms that are seen as part of the disorder such as depressed mood, high levels of panic and anxiety and self-harming behaviours, but they do not feel there is any treatment for the disorder as a whole.

This sort of 'diagnosis' and 'treatment' rarely makes any woman feel better and often only increases the feelings of exclusion and isolation that lead to the need to self-harm in the first place.

They say I'm personality disordered, yet another label telling me what I am. Even worse they say *'it's* not amenable to treatment' as if *it's* not me or if it is me then I am not a person. I walk out of the office, I was in there for 7½ minutes; amazing that a whole life can be pronounced upon in 7½ minutes. I feel like a worthless waste of space and time, why would anyone waste their time with me.

Tyler

It is now understood by those who work with adult survivors of childhood trauma, particularly if the trauma is repeated sexual abuse,[3] that those characteristics that are deemed to be evidence of a 'personality disorder' are predictable and normal human responses to such trauma.[4] So symptoms *are* amenable to treatment – not through medical intervention, but by exploration of the original trauma.

Marsha Linehan who works therapeutically with women who have been given the label BPD, reports that almost all of her clients have experienced what she terms an 'invalidating environment' where personal experience is denied or disqualified particularly by those who played a parental role during the woman's early life.[5] Marsha Linehan and others also propose that there are physiological characteristics that make some individuals more likely to react to the invalidating environment.[6] These individuals are thought to have an autonomic nervous system that reacts dramatically to stress and takes a long time to return to normal after any stressful experience. An explanation that combines both a biological predisposition and environmental factors that come together to create a particular difficulty is called a diathesis stress model. It is useful in helping to understand, for instance, why only one child from an abusive family might develop self-harming behaviour, whilst the others, who may also have experienced the same abusive early childhood do not.

This is important for carers of anyone who self-harms. Although it may seem strange that one person has responded to an abusive situation by self-harming whereas another seems to show little or no overt disturbance at all, this difference could be explained by their different physiological makeup.

Schizophrenia

In our society, schizophrenia is the psychiatric label that epitomises madness. However it is not a single disorder, but is a name given to what appears to be a whole range of disorders in which a person seems to have a very different sense of reality than that which is believed by others to be the norm. People who are given a diagnosis of schizophrenia often exhibit with several of the following features:

a) Disorders of thought: one stream of thought suddenly stops and another continues; belief that thoughts are being broadcast or inserted; delusions such as that of being persecuted, or of omnipotence; delusions about different parts of the body.
b) Disorders of perception: auditory hallucinations – hearing voices or noises; visual hallucinations (rare); bodily hallucinations – feeling heat, cold, pain and also sexual sensations; hallucinations of smell and taste.
c) Emotional disorder: depression; anxiety; a complete flattening of emotion or emotion that does not fit the situation the person is experiencing.
d) Disorder of behaviour: feelings that thoughts and/or speech are not the person's own and have been implanted by external influences; long periods of not moving; agitated behaviours such as tearing, wandering or senseless moaning.

Labelling people who have such symptoms as 'mad', is a very unhelpful and mistaken attitude. Often these 'symptoms' are the means the person has found whereby they can communicate something extremely painful, something about which they have been unable to speak openly.

Many women who are given a diagnosis of schizophrenia do self-harm, often in extremely severe ways. They frequently say that they have done so in response to instructions from the voices in their head, or as a result of delusions, particularly delusions with a religious or sexual content. In our experience, after building up some trust, many of these women eventually begin to describe having suffered multiple traumas in childhood and it can then be seen that the majority of the symptoms are responses to those traumas. When the fact that they have experienced a trauma is known, some of their apparently delusional thoughts and behaviours are recognised as being related to their actual experience, therefore they are not truly delusional.

For example, some women have told us that they self-harm in response to 'voices in my head' which could be labelled as being 'auditory hallucinations' and thus be part of the diagnosis of schizophrenia. When the woman is asked to talk more about these voices, it often becomes clear that they are really a part of herself, or voices of people who have been important in her life, frequently childhood abusers. These voices tend to say derogatory things about the woman. Some of these things may have been said to her directly when she was being abused. Others will be messages she will have picked up because of what was done to her. These communications become almost concrete and are repeated over and over again in her head like a mantra. Often there is one voice which 'tells' the woman to hurt herself and sometimes another which tries to protect her. If hearing voices in your head is part of your experience, trying to develop a stronger more protective voice is really important.

At times it would be constant. It was his voice saying over and over to me, 'You're a slut.' 'You're a whore.' 'You love it don't you.' 'You're crap.' 'You're just a piece of shit.' 'So what if it hurts, you deserve to be hurt, you deserve to be punished.' I'd get really really agitated and the only way to shut him up was to cut or burn myself. Once I'd damaged myself, his voice stopped for a while. It seemed like if I punished myself, he'd be satisfied for a while.

Sheena

Body hallucinations are another 'symptom' or 'feature' of schizophrenia that women often describe leads them to self-harm. Yet what appear to be 'bodily hallucinations' could be 'body memories' of the trauma that the women have endured. These are actual physical sensations that are associated with the original trauma: pain in the vagina and anus; feelings of penetration and associated sexual arousal; feelings of choking and gagging; feelings of a body on top of theirs and of the skin of the abuser on their skin; feeling pain in their body as if it had recently been beaten; bodily feelings associated with repeated childhood surgery that at the time may not have been felt due to anaesthesia. This can lead to desperate attempts to rid the body of these unpleasant feelings.

> I can feel her on my skin...I can't explain...I suppose it's like...as if we are in some way we are melted into each other. I scrape and scrape at my skin but I cannot get deep enough into myself to get rid of her.
>
> Linda

Women who have 'voices in their head' and 'body hallucinations' say that they are often too scared to talk about them. They say that they worry that telling anyone about these experiences will confirm that they are 'mad'. However, if you can begin to trust someone with your innermost thoughts and feelings, even those that seem frightening and strange, you, and the person in whom you confide, can help make sense of it all, and your need to self-harm may reduce considerably.

> I'd been in enough hospitals to know that if they knew that you heard voices in your head, they'd say you were psychotic, mad. I was terrified if I told anyone they'd say I was mad. The problem is that *I* thought that it meant I was mad too. Just hearing them go on and on at me, made me want to cut. It was only when

I really began to trust my foster mother and tell her about them and she did not think I was mad. In fact it made me realise that they were just repeating all the things that my mother and brother had said to me over the years; that's when I realised I wasn't mad. Most people have these sorts of thoughts in their head, I just hear mine as voices because they hurt me so badly. So I learnt to argue with them, to tell them to 'piss off', that they were wrong and that they would say that to justify how badly they treated me. They've backed down a lot. I don't hear them anywhere near as much as I used to. They still wind me up a bit sometimes but much less than they did and so I cut less than I did. I used to cut as it shut them up.

Tyler

Psychological Explanations

There are several possible explanations that therapists, counsellors and academic psychologists suggest in order to understand self-harming behaviour. However, it is crucial that you are allowed to make your own sense of what your behaviour means to you rather than being given someone else's interpretation. Each of us is the expert on ourselves and our feelings. A therapist is there to help provide a space and a framework within which you can come to an understanding of your own individual experience. The same is true of the following examples of common explanations for self-harm. These are meant to provide a space within which you can consider their relevance to your own situation and feelings.

Coping with Emotional Tension

Many women who self-harm tell us they do so in order to relieve emotional tension. This tension often arises from the experience of trauma in early life. The actual emotions they most frequently describe are anxiety, agitation and anger. The emotional tension increases to such a pitch that women describe not being able to tolerate these feelings or control them. As we have stated, no human being can tolerate being in a high state of emotional tension for any length of time. We have to do something to deflate the high level of emotional arousal so that we can carry on with our lives. It may be that at some time in the past self-harm has provided relief of the tension and anxiety. If this has been the case, it may be hard to think of anything else to do other than self-harm to bring about feelings of relief.

This preoccupation intensifies and women describe beginning to include reasons as to why they *should* self-harm. Feelings of self-loathing and low self-esteem can fuel the justification that hurting yourself is the only way to relieve the tension. Women describe feeling little if any pain while they are harming themselves even though the injuries at times can be quite severe. They also describe stopping the self-harming behaviour when they feel either a release, or a change in mood. The sensation of pain may not return for some time after the injury; in some cases not for hours or days.

Once I let myself decide to do it, the relief seems to begin. I sort of go into a bit of a haze, I do things sort of automatically. I go out to buy my blades, tissues, bandages and melanin strips. I've got hundreds of blades at home but I like to get new ones each time, it's part of it. I think about what I'm going to do, where, how I'm going to do it. It's all part of it. I then go to the bathroom, sit on the mat and take everything out of the wrappers and place them all around me in the same order. I break the razors and by then I already feel much better, much calmer.

Sarah

This 'relief' is usually only temporary. Self-harming behaviour cannot remove the cause of the emotional pressure and so when anything happens that triggers negative feelings, and the level of arousal builds up, the woman will feel the need to self-harm again. In this way self-harm can become part of a cycle of behaviour. Some women find that over time, the injuries they inflict on themselves have to become more severe in order to achieve the same degree of relief.

Some women who self-harm say that they do so as they cannot express their feelings in any other way. They describe being desperate to communicate how they feel but being unable to do so, and resorting to self-harm to relieve the feelings of frustration that inability causes. Bonnie Burstow describes this process:

> They desperately need to communicate, yet they cannot because they do not feel entitled to speak about the pain or to ask for help. Moreover, they are not certain that anyone would heed them if they did, and they cannot afford to risk further rejection. Their solution is to communicate indirectly. THEY CREATE WOUNDS THAT SPEAK FOR THEM. In their own way they are reaching out...Ashamed both of reaching out generally and of reaching out in this particular way many women hide their wounds intended to communicate. They put the wounds in places where they cannot be seen. Often a hint of the wound is present, for this conflicted woman still wants to be seen.[7]
>
> Burstow

Self-harm is thus seen as a symptom of internal distress which has both a private and a public message.

Dissociative States

Another way that we find of dealing with serious emotional distress when there is no care or comfort available to us is by completely cutting off those emotions and associated events – dissociating. This is most likely to happen when a young child has experienced a very severe trauma. This is not a conscious act; it is a way in which our minds protect us from unbearable pain and terror. It is like a state of self-generated hypnosis. At a later time, triggers associated with this original trauma can unconsciously lead to a similar dissociative state. A dissociative state leaves a person with a feeling of deadness and disconnection from others. Many women talk about feeling 'cut-off' as if they might 'just drift out of existence and never come back', or 'numb' 'totally blank' or 'not there' before self-harming.

It's as if it isn't me doing it, I'm just watching it 'being done'.

Tyler

Judith Herman describes how children who dissociate learn that this dissociative state can be ended by 'a major jolt to the body', thus to inflict an injury on yourself may be a means of reconnecting with the real world.[9]

If you have no recollection of an episode of self-harm or have a very firm belief that it wasn't you who inflicted the injuries you now see or feel, but actually on another level know that it must have been, it is likely that when you hurt yourself you were in an altered state of consciousness, in other words – dissociated.

Each time I'd go to casualty with my cuts it would be the same questions. Did you do this yourself? Did anyone force you to do it? Was anyone with you when you did it? What did you use? Were you trying to kill yourself? I got so sick of telling them – I did it to myself, no one except myself forced me to do it. I was alone. I used a razor blade and OF COURSE I WASN'T TRYING TO KILL MYSELF...I WAS TRYING TO MAKE MYSELF FEEL ALIVE...

Sheena

Anger Directed to Self

It is thought that when children do not have their needs appropriately met or are actively abused, they develop a very powerful anger as a protest. Children, especially girls, are often punished for any expression of anger, and so this anger becomes repressed. Even as we get older, females in our society are socialised not to express their anger.

Overwhelming angry feelings against a powerful significant person in your life such as a parental figure can feel excruciating. If you can no longer hold these angry feelings 'in' and you have been socialised not to express them outwardly, this anger may become directed inwards on your self.

> At times I rage at the brutal existence forced on me
> I want to scream and shout in protest
> but it all stays inside, hurting
> Furious tears struggle to flow
> I prevent them in case I should lose control
> Self-mutilation is an outlet
> watching my blood flow, feeling nothing
> Silent red tears of rage and anguish
>
> Tyler

Self-Punishment

As women, we are often made to feel guilty about our feelings, particularly angry feelings (as mentioned above). Some women use self-harm as a punishment for experiencing emotions that they feel they should not have, and in a strange way this seems to relieve their guilt. Women often justify directing anger at themselves because of perceived feelings of failure and inadequacy, often related to relationship difficulties. This is a particularly female trait with women taking a greater degree of responsibility for maintaining relationships than men. Many women who self-harm describe growing up in families where even as young children they have been made to feel responsible for everything, including maintaining a good relationship with their parents.

> My mother never seemed to like me. Nothing I did seemed to please her. She never cared what happened to me. I'm sure she knew he was raping me but she did nothing. I must have done something to cause her such hatred. It must have been my fault just as it is my fault that all my relationships fail, why I'm all alone. Now she's dead and I can never make the relationship between us right. I'm so angry at myself. Why didn't I sort it out before she died?

Sarah

Many survivors of childhood abuse take on the beliefs of those who perpetrated the abuse against them. This can take the form of feeling that they were the 'bad', 'evil' ones, and either 'wanted' or 'deserved' what had happened to them when they were children. As they have taken on the beliefs of the perpetrator that 'it was your fault'; 'you are to blame'; it is not difficult to see how the anger becomes directed inwards and how they come to see hurting their own bodies as a form of punishment. Ironically, the self-harm itself seems like further confirmation of the woman's inherent badness, worthlessness and need for punishment. If the abuser has fetishised any part of the woman's body, they may particularly attack that part, because they feel as if it is responsible for the abuse.

> Even when I was only three or four he'd say I had such lovely breasts. It was so sick, he kept talking about how they'd grow and how lovely they would be. I'd hate him touching them so much. Whenever I cut myself, wherever I cut, I always did one cut there. It was always the first cut I did.

Lucy

Some women who have experienced sexual abuse in childhood feel intense anger and guilt because their bodies reacted normally to sexual stimulation and they became sexually aroused during the abusive interaction. This does not mean they wanted the sexual abuse to happen or that they enjoyed it. It just means their bodies responded as bodies are programmed to do. This may cause difficulties later when sexual arousal during consensual experiences becomes a trigger to aversive memories including traumatic flashbacks. This can lead to self-harming behaviour which may sometimes be directed specifically towards genitals.

Survivor Guilt

Witnessing terrible violence is a traumatic event which can have a profound impact on a woman's life. It can lead to 'survivor guilt' – powerful feelings of helplessness and guilt that you were not the one who was hurt. You can feel as if you were 'bad' because you 'let it happen', and guilty because you didn't get hurt or were not hurt as badly as others were. Women who as children have watched their mothers being beaten can 'beat' themselves up, both emotionally and physically. The negative impact of domestic violence on children, even if they have not been hit, is now beginning to be recognised.[10]

Punishing Someone Else

Self-harming behaviour can also be a means of showing someone, usually family members or others who have hurt you, that you *are* hurt and that damage has been done.

> I needed to cut myself. The bigger and deeper the cut the better. I just wanted to show them how much I hurt. How much they hurt me.
>
> Lucy

Some women who have been traumatised in childhood, can feel 'as if the perpetrator is inside of them'. In such a case an episode of self-harm may be an attempt to hurt the abuser within or make the abuser come out.

> I hate her so much, my whole body sometimes feels explosive when I think of her or even if someone mentions the word mother. I can't get her away from me, she is with me day and night. She lives and breathes me. I feel her inside and out. When I inhale I feel she fills even more of me. When I exhale, I feel that the breath I breathe is infected with her, so I try not to breathe on anyone in case they are made bad by her breath. There is no way away from her, she is with me day and night. The torment is killing me. I sometimes think people can see my mother inside me. I feel entwined by her, my body still feels connected to hers. I feel covered and smothered by her. I want to hurt her, kill her. I cut her flesh away from mine. It is the only way that I will be free of her
>
> Claire

Re-enactment of Aspects of the Trauma

Some therapists such as Gloria Babiker and Lois Arnold see significance in the fact that virtually all self-injury involves breaking the skin.[11] They describe how starting in infancy a whole range of emotions are communicated via skin contact or lack of it. Washing, stroking, soothing, holding, and warmth all involve sensations within the skin. Neglect of a child often leaves the child feeling physically uncomfortable, wet, cold, sore. Traumas of many kinds, particularly those which have occurred in childhood, involve a breaking of the skin or a breaching of the physical boundaries which are delineated by the skin. Babiker and Arnold suggest that acts of self-harm may be a re-enactment of these violations in an attempt to understand or resolve the experience. Dusty Miller refers to this as the 'Trauma Re-enactment Syndrome'.[12] She believes that the woman is doing to her body something that represents what was done to her as a child.

Often after an episode of self-harm, the skin is soothed and cared for. This comforting, needed to repair the damage, did not occur in response to the original trauma but in occurring in the present becomes a reparation for past failures.

The Addiction Model: Biological Effects of Self-Harm

All of our behaviour brings about changes within the central nervous system of our bodies. Self-harm is no exception. The following is a simplified description that describes some, but by no means all, of the changes that occur as a result.

Any aspect of behaviour is regulated by a range of chemicals found within the brain called neurochemicals. There is evidence that the group of neurochemicals known as endogenous opioids and another neurochemical called serotonin have a role to play in self-harm.

Endogenous opioids are neurochemicals, similar to the drugs opium and heroin, which bring about a very positive feeling of calm and well-being. These endogenous opioids are released when a person feels in danger, experiences fear and particularly when the body is injured in any way. They produce an insensitivity to pain which will help the person survive when having to deal with danger. Thus during trauma of any kind, a woman's body will release endogenous opioids to protect against possible pain and increase the likelihood of survival.

At a later time anything – a smell, a sound, a taste, an image, a feeling – that triggers a woman into re-experiencing overwhelming feelings will lead to a release of endogenous opioids. We can become addicted to our own endogenous opioids and therefore need more to be released in order to bring about a feeling of calm. Ways may have to be found of inducing the body to release more and one way of doing this is by self-harming. After self-harm there can be a feeling of release, calm and pleasure. Also as endogenous opioids are natural painkillers, this may explain why some women say they feel no pain during, and for some time after, they have hurt themselves.

In this way self-harm can become a repetitive cycle. As with other physical addictions, it is possible to suffer from withdrawal from your own endogenous opioids. This physical withdrawal may increase feelings of bodily tension and the urge to self-harm may seem 'almost uncontrollable'.

In addition when someone is subjected to high levels of stress, they have lowered levels of the neurotransmitter, serotonin. Low levels of serotonin are linked with various kinds of impulsive behaviour and lack of constraint, so it becomes difficult to resist the urge to self-harm. As the body begins to build up a tolerance to endogenous opioids, a greater level of harm may have to be inflicted to achieve the same effect.

While there are clear bodily feelings that may trigger self-harming behaviour, these are closely associated with thoughts, emotions and feelings about yourself and others in your life.

Making Use Of These Explanations

Both women who self-harm, people who care for them and professionals who work with them, attribute various meanings and communications to the behaviour itself. All too often the numerous views regarding why a woman self-harms mean that the personal and individual significance of self-harm can go unheard. When our beliefs and emotions are not confirmed or validated by others in our lives, we feel alienated and disconnected, and we begin to feel that our views and perceptions are abnormal or mad.

Through talking and sharing our experiences, we can begin to receive affirmation and validation of our own reality. If there is a common understanding about what is happening when an episode of self-harm occurs, the possibility of changing and of finding other ways of managing stress and distress is much more likely.

Thinking through possible reasons you self-harm is a very positive personal step you can take towards that goal. Overcoming trauma and pain is a long and difficult process but there are many different forms of help available. It is important that you find out what is on offer so that you can make the decision which is right for you.

Chapter 3
Getting Access to Services

In the course of researching this book, we wrote to every provider of National Health Care in this country to ask them about the services they provide for women who self-harm. We received few replies and of those only a very small number described any specialist services. Most said women who self-harm would be dealt with within their normal psychiatric services, or if the women requested a specialist service they would be referred to voluntary organisations.

'Normal psychiatric services', of course, vary greatly from region to region, so it is helpful to know the range of possibilities you may be offered should you access the National Health Service. The following two chapters aim to provide you with information about the many sorts of help that are available so that if you do approach conventional services, you will be able to make a more informed choice as to whether or not to accept the treatment proposed. You may prefer to ask for a referral to someone who can offer a treatment which better suits your needs.

The personal opinion of the referrer or individual to whom you are referred will tend to determine the treatment you are offered. Broadly speaking, professionals who see self-harm as part of a psychiatric disorder are primarily likely to offer medication. If this is ineffective, in some severe cases ECT may be suggested and in very rare cases psychosurgery.

Those who see it as 'attention-seeking' behaviour, as being manipulative or as part of a learned behaviour pattern will probably refer you to a behaviourally based programme. These may be carried out by behaviour therapists, community psychiatric nurses or clinical psychologists.

If the professional feels that your self-harm is primarily a response to a traumatic event they are liable to recommend therapy to help you process your traumatic experiences. Many professionals use a combination of various treatments, hoping to offer the best chance of success.

The service you receive will also depend on the referral route. You can access conventional health services via three main routes: self-referral, General Practitioners (GPs), and Accident and Emergency Departments.

Self-Referral

Conventional sources of help can be obtained from both the private and the National Health services. If you want to self-refer to a private therapist of any kind, for your own safety, do make sure the person has recognised qualifications and is connected to a professional association.[1]

There have been many changes in the health service over recent years which have meant that it has become increasingly difficult, and in some areas impossible, for a person to refer themselves directly to a specific professional or source of help. If you know what you want, you need to research your local resources to find out who you think may be able to provide it within the health service.

Within the National Health Service there is often a lack of specific resources for women who self-harm. Additionally, there is increasing pressure within the service to limit the number of sessions offered to any one client.[2] However, 'going private' does not necessarily guarantee a better service.

> I tried NHS help and found it to be no help at all, as, in the main its staff had no idea how to treat me. Then I tried private psychotherapy which was extremely costly and very upsetting. It dragged a lot of unpleasant things to the surface of my mind and when my therapist discovered that I was a self-harmer she immediately dumped me for fear I might accidentally kill myself. She left me in a state of turmoil which took ages to undo.
>
> Dee

Researching what is available locally is not easy. Health Trusts should have brochures and leaflets describing services they provide but this is not always the case. Even when these are available they may not be very detailed or are out-of-date.

General Practitioner (GP)

In many cases your GP may be the best source of accurate local information. If you have a good relationship with your GP, you should say what it is you feel you need, and ask if he or she knows any service that may be able to provide it. This is not always an easy thing to do and you might want to write down what you want prior to going to the GP. If you go without stating what help you want, you will most likely be given whatever help fits in with the GP's own beliefs as to why you self-harm.

I first asked for help in August last year. I was depressed and could not stop thinking about cutting so I wrote to my GP. She wrote back saying she could help. She suggested a counsellor and put me on antidepressants.

Elaine

Accident and Emergency Departments (A&E)

One of the most common points of entry women who self-harm have to other health services is when they attend Accident and Emergency Departments with their injuries. If on admission any further referral is to be made, it is usually directed towards psychiatric services. In A&E, a woman normally receives only physical care for the injury and is then sent home with no follow-up, unless the episode is considered to be 'life-threatening behaviour'. Even so, what you consider to be life threatening may not even raise an eyebrow in the casualty department.

The total indifference I received at the hospital was shocking. I sat in an ambulance with a blade in my hand and no one took it off me or even acknowledged it was there. In hospital, no one checked my bag. I had 60 blades and pills in it.

Christine

Many women who self-harm feel they are treated so badly in accident and emergency departments that they would only go for treatment if it was absolutely necessary and would discharge themselves the minute they had received basic first-aid.

Going to A & E became another form of self-harm where the staff's judgement confirmed for me that I was the lowest form of life and reinforced every negative feeling I ever had about myself.[3]

If, however, it is felt that you are at risk of killing

yourself you are likely to be referred to the duty psychiatrist. The treatment, physical and emotional, you then receive will again depend on his or her interpretation of what self-harm means. As we have seen, most psychiatrists believe that self-harm stems from a psychiatric illness or is a form of attention-seeking behaviour. Going to Accident and Emergency following a serious episode of self-harm is the most common way that women who cause deliberate injury to themselves get admitted to in-patient services.

In-patient Treatment

The quality of in-patient treatment you can expect to receive is again very dependent on the philosophy of the unit and the individual staff working within that unit. In *The Language of Injury*, Gloria Babiker and Lois Arnold describe how women who self-harm often go into hospital for real 'asylum'; a place of safety, help and respite.[4] Unfortunately that is rarely the case. Wards often mix male and female clients together. Even if you do manage to be on an all-female ward there are invariably male staff. Whether they are staff or other clients, the very presence of men in such an environment can be a trigger for some women, especially those who have experienced sexual abuse in their childhood. In the worst cases, it can reinforce many aspects of the original trauma. One woman even describes being sexually assaulted while she was in hospital.

> The tension was building up and I knew I was going to cut myself. I went to get help from a member of staff. The female member of staff on duty was on her break so there was only a male nurse there. I told him how I felt and he suggested that I masturbate to release the tension. I couldn't speak, my mind was instantly filled with images of the sexual assaults I had endured

throughout my childhood. I thought my mind would explode. I walked out of the office. Later that evening I woke up to find the male nurse standing over me with his hand on my genitals.

Ann

Many women say that they feel so helpless and controlled by the staff, that their feelings of frustration intensify and again become turned inward on to the self. Some women describe being triggered into further episodes of self-harm in this way.

I searched the hospital grounds for glass and did the worst cuts I've ever done...it felt like anger at the nurses, doctors and myself...the nurses dressed my cuts and were very impatient with me.

Patricia

The philosophy of most psychiatric wards can reinforce painful feelings for women who self-harm. As Gloria Babiker and Lois Arnold discuss, the woman is seen as 'ill', and is there to be 'made better'; the cure for emotional distress is usually an immediate physical solution (medication); the woman's movements and choices tend to be controlled and closely observed thus taking away her personal responsibility; if she does not comply she is seen as 'bad' and needing to be 'contained'.[5]

A survey was carried out asking nurses and junior doctors to rate clients they found most difficult. Self-harm was considered to be one of the characteristics of their most difficult clients. They described how, when caring for these clients, they began to feel helpless and often felt actively angry and resentful towards them.

It is very hard for others to cope with. In my experience most ignore what's happening because it frightens them and perhaps it reminds them of their own self-destructive tendencies.

Christina

To deal with these feelings of helplessness in professionals, women who self-harm often become reduced to labels such as 'cutters' and 'harmers' which maintains a distance between the professionals and clients – a distance that protects the professional at the woman's expense. Most women can sense when staff's attitude is hostile and this increases feelings of rejection and alienation. Often 'cures' offered while an inpatient can seem more like punishments and do nothing to build up feelings of self-worth.

Additionally professional staff are not encouraged to be tactile often due to the fear that such contact may be seen as intrusive or may be otherwise misinterpreted as abuse. However, all of us, particularly when we feel vulnerable and distressed need comfort, understanding, reassurance and continuity from those who are caring for us. When hospitalised those in that role are the staff.

> When I harmed myself, I didn't want people to see the outward signs of my inner hurt but I did want love and cuddles to demonstrate to me that I wasn't hateful and unlovable.
>
> Dee

Some professionals identify so many problems with inpatient treatment that they recommend that a person who self-harms is never admitted to hospital unless there is a specialist treatment unit with informed and trained staff.[6]

However, some women do receive beneficial care and support in hospital, usually because they have developed good trusting relationships with particular members of staff.

> There was this staff called Jean, she was all right, I could talk to her. Once when she was on nights I went to her and told her that I wanted to cut or burn myself. She asked me if she could touch my hand and my arm. I said yes and she just stroked me, calmly, up and down

my hand and my arm, up and down. She talked to me. Told me to close my eyes and to imagine a chaotic place, bustling and full of people and noise and then she told me to think of walking away from there and described a walk that took me in my mind to a quiet peaceful place. I couldn't believe it, the need to cut went away. I told another staff, Michele, who I got on with, what Jean had done and asked her if she would do it when Jean wasn't on duty. It didn't always work but the more that I did it the better it seemed to work. Then I realised that for the first time for more than 10 years, a whole week had gone by and I hadn't cut or burnt myself.

Sheena

If more staff could be trained to understand and respond empathetically to women who self-harm then being in hospital would be a more effective form of help.

Out-Patient Treatment

In-patient services in themselves are unlikely to provide a 'cure'. Follow up is absolutely essential, otherwise many of the improvements you may have made while in hospital may not be sustained in the community.

Discharge from hospital was planned even though they knew I didn't feel comfortable with leaving. I felt unwanted and alone. They wanted me out of hospital and they would have me out. I have no faith in the local mental health unit. I feel there is no one to turn to.

Elaine

Often the amount of professional time is dramatically reduced. So you can go from total supervision to very brief appointments.

My Community Psychiatric Nurse (CPN) came to see me last week...but she only stayed 20 minutes.

Sharon

However, this is not always the case. Some women feel they are offered less of a service while in-patients then they received as out-patients.

Eventually it was decided I needed a psychiatrist. We got nowhere in relation to my self-harm until I told him about the drink. I was admitted to the unit and given more tablets. But I saw *more* of my psychiatrist as an out-patient than I did as an in-patient.

Elaine

The doctor with most regular contact is almost always a registrar – a junior doctor in training. As the doctors rotate through their training programme placements, any trusting relationships that have been formed during the 'rotation' will be disrupted.

I was given a six-week course of ECT and a new female psychiatrist suddenly uncovered the abuse by asking the right questions. I spent a long time being counselled. Then disaster struck – she left. I felt I'd been left on a desert island. I hated her replacement, and the anorexia and self-harm returned with a vengeance.

Susanne

These moves occur every six months for junior registrars and yearly for senior registrars. Many of the other professionals involved in your care will also be on training programmes and 'rotating' through a particular placement. This includes clinical psychologists, nurses (community psychiatric nurses – CPNs; behaviour therapists) and Occupational Therapists (OTs).

There were too many faces. I am a private person who needs one to one relationships. Even the psychiatrists change around every six months.

Elaine

Often there is a shortfall of resources to help you with the transition from hospital into the community. Some women are lucky and are provided with housing that offers additional support and may even include someone who regularly checks that you are managing on your own and is readily available if you become distressed. In the absence of such transitional schemes, hospitalisation can be part of a revolving door with brief admissions following especially severe episodes where you are patched up, and 'detained' for a while, and then the inevitable discharge home to manage as best you can. One of the risks of hospitalisation is the possibility that you might be detained against your wishes.

Compulsory Hospitalisation

If you are deemed to be a danger to yourself and to others, or are suffering from a 'mental disorder', you can be detained compulsorily in hospital. 'Mental Disorder' is defined under the Mental Health Act as: mental illness, arrested or incomplete development of mind, psychopathic disorder and any other disorder or disability of the mind. Consequently it seems that interpretation of this term still depends a great deal on the doctor who is making it.

You can be detained on a:

- Section 4 for 72 hours for emergency assessment
- Section 2 for 28 days for assessment with or without treatment
- Section 3 for 6 months for treatment (which needs to be renewed after 6 months and then yearly)

Application for detention can be from your nearest relative or an Approved Social Worker. Section 4 is considered an emergency Section and only one doctor needs to examine you and make the recommendation you should be detained. Sections 2 and 3 require you to be examined by two doctors, one of whom has had 'previous acquaintance' with you, and both need to recommend that you be detained under the Section.

If you are already in hospital voluntarily, for whatever reason, you can be detained compulsorily by the doctor in charge of your care for 72 hours, during which further powers of detention can be applied for. If there is no doctor immediately available to detain you a specifically designated psychiatric nurse can hold you against your will for a maximum of six hours until a doctor arrives. This whole process can be very frightening, especially if you do not feel it is necessary.

If you cannot get the medical staff to understand why you do not think a Section would be useful, you should try and explain your position to the Approved Social Worker who may be able to prevent the Section from being made. If you are admitted under a Section, you have the right to apply to a Mental Health Review Tribunal for discharge. You can also be discharged by your nearest relative, the managers of the hospital or the Responsible Medical Officer (usually your consultant psychiatrist). However your relative can be barred from discharging you by the Responsible Medical Officer if he or she deems you to be dangerous. If you find yourself in this kind of a situation, it is best to contact an advocacy service to help you put your point of view across.[7] You should have a strong case regarding hospitalisation as research suggests that whatever the regime of a particular unit, it is at best a very temporary solution to self-harm. However, it will also depend a great deal on how seriously you are injuring yourself.

An Alternative Model of Hospital Treatment

One European hospital carries out what appears to be a very different approach to people who harm themselves by cutting, scraping, burning, and applying chemicals to their skin.[8] This self-harm is understood as a means of reducing tension and the addictive nature of the behaviour is recognised. Clients are treated in the ward that is related to the physical injuries they sustained rather than in psychiatric wards, but there is close communication between staff teams. The client is given medical care for their injuries; bandages, creams, and painkillers, and although drugs may be given to reduce tension the limit of their effectiveness is recognised. The importance of a long-standing trusting relationship with medical staff is clearly acknowledged. This system seems to have proved to be a very effective form of treatment.

Chapter 4
Conventional Treatments

Your consent should always be sought for any treatment you receive. This includes all forms of medication and other physical treatments such as electroconvulsive therapy (ECT). Your informed consent should also be obtained for any psychological therapy you become involved in. Good practice should involve discussing what treatments are available, what each entails and any possible side effects, so that you can give informed consent before commencing.

If the treatment occurs under a Section, it must be certified that you have given your consent and that you fully understand what it involves. If while on a Section you are offered a treatment which you don't consent to, an independent doctor will be called to ascertain whether you understand the nature and purpose of the treatment and whether it is necessary for you to be given it. You may be feeling vulnerable and confused, and may not be in a position to refuse the treatments offered to you.

At one stage of Tyler's 'treatment' for self-harming behaviour she was being prescribed *all at the one time*, on a daily basis Doxepin (antidepressant), Valium (anti-anxiety), Thioridazine (major tranquilliser), Chloral hydrate (sedative prescribed as a sleeping pill). She was still regularly self-harming so was hospitalised and given a course of ECT – a week after her last 'treatment' while she was still in hospital she cut her leg so badly she needed more than 50 stitches in the wounds. She was discharged after a ward round as the consultant psychiatrist said she was *non-compliant* with treatment!

Carer

Physical Treatments

Medication

Almost all women who have approached medical professionals have, at some time, been prescribed at least one form of drug therapy. Although some of these drugs are more helpful than others, there is no evidence that any currently available medication can consistently control self-harming behaviour.

Even those drugs which do have some positive effect will only be a temporary solution if nothing is done to look at the underlying problems that lead you to self-harm.

> You just don't understand how terrible these urges are to rip at my flesh. It's constant now. I used to cut to feel in control, now I feel the need to cut controls me. The release from these feelings after I've cut lasts no time now. The urges return very quickly. I know medication is a temporary solution to the constant urges but I feel that I need something.
>
> Debbie

In addition all these forms of medication have side effects, some of which are very unpleasant. A detailed list of the most usual drugs prescribed is provided at the end of the book in the References and Resources section. The list describes the major drug groups and their side effects.

If you feel alienated from your body, taking these drugs over long periods of time maintains the estrangement that you feel through chemical distortion; you can feel tired even when you have slept all night. The feedback your body is giving you is mediated through a drug-induced haze. On the one hand this may be exactly what you are looking for, but in the longer term, this type of treatment does not help you to learn your body's signals for distress, tiredness, hunger, thirst and your emotions can become muffled.

> I was told I looked so much 'better' on neuroleptic drugs but the reality was different for me. In fact their effects, such as emotional blunting merely made self-harming easier as pain and fear are dulled.[1]

Medication can exacerbate your difficulty in recognising and understanding how you feel. It can also interfere with your ability to communicate your emotions. It often makes other people feel better about you partially by stifling any attempt to make your true feelings known to them.

> Each day they give me a large amount of drugs, tablets that are supposed to make me feel better. They think I'm better because I've stopped slashing myself but inside I'm worse. But I remain silent. I sit quietly, feeling dead inside, dull vacant eyes, looking around but not really seeing anything, with no energy to see anything. Strangely detached, everything is meaningless. Even the screams in my head are silent. I have become passive, accepting this as my life. It's ironic I take tablets that make me feel dead in order that I can stay alive.
>
> Tyler

Electroconvulsive Therapy (ECT)

If a woman does not respond to medication, medical professionals who consider self-harm to be a symptom of severe depression may consider the use of ECT. Although exactly what happens within the brain when ECT is given is not known, it is still regarded by many in the psychiatric services to be an effective and useful treatment. ECT involves the brief passing of an electric current through electrodes placed on the head in order to induce a convulsion. A sedative and relaxant are given to ensure that no bones are broken.

A course of treatment usually entails two convulsions a week for approximately 6 weeks. There is, however, no evidence at all that this is effective in reducing self-harming behaviour and any improvement seems to be short-term. As with all medication, it is treating the symptoms without looking for the cause. It also has side effects which include confusion and memory loss. It is often stated that these side effects are temporary, but in practice they can last for weeks, months and in some cases become permanent.

> I feel so confused, unsure of what I am doing, what I want, what I need – are those two things the same? Are drugs the solution? They mask the symptoms, they numb my brain, they are not a cure but I take them to get through the day. I go into hospital when it gets too much. I even let them give me electric shocks in the desperate hope it will take away the feelings that the drugs can't. It sometimes feels as though they hurt the inside of my body to stop me hurting the outside of my body – I'm just so confused.
>
> Tyler

Women's Reactions to Psychiatric Services

Maggie Ross, a survivor of self-harm, sexual abuse and *psychiatric treatment* [our emphasis]...one of the founder members of the Bristol Crisis Service for Women...campaigner...died in her struggle...but she knew that whenever a person gained their voice, it is a victory for all of us. That each time a person is incarcerated it is an indictment of our society, not their mental state.[2]

The women we have spoken to on the whole felt very dissatisfied with the psychiatric services that have been offered. In fact the government do recognise this and have actually stated that *'qualified staff needed supplementary training to deal with deliberate self-harm'*.[3] However, women's dissatisfaction with psychiatric services is not restricted to the ways that they deal with self-harm – women who use psychiatric services for other reasons have also registered dissatisfaction with the help they have received.[4] Some women have had repeated bad experiences. They say that as each inappropriate treatment fails, feelings of hopelessness set in and they feel more and more pathologised.

Age 15 – Parents took her to the GP; GP referral to psychiatrist; hospital admission. Given aversion therapy [!]

Age 16 – given tranquillisers

Age 18 – admitted to acute ward; given Largactil and ECT

Age 20 – referred for hypnotherapy; 6 months later in locked ward

Age 21 – she refused treatment; overdosed; 6 month stay in psychiatric hospital

Age 26 – given further drugs, MAOI, Lithium and Melleril

Age 36 – admitted back on drugs

Age 38 – referred to clinical psychologist but was told too emotionally damaged for her to help

Theresa

There is a growing voice among women, clearly articulating their need for a different approach to the problem of self-harm. Recently, there have been an increasing number of national conferences addressing the issue both within mental health and the prison system. This reflects a burgeoning awareness among professionals that they too must think carefully about the issues involved and, indeed, many conferences have recognised that conventional treatment is not as effective as it could be.

Psychological Treatments

Although the distinction between psychiatric and psychological treatments is not clearly demarcated, there is overwhelming evidence from consumers of mental health services that they would like to have more 'talking therapies'. These include a broad range of approaches, from just listening to more formal psychotherapies.

In a survey commissioned by the Mental Health Foundation, the authors, all service users themselves, indicated that clients should be seen as the primary experts on themselves.[5] They endorsed a more holistic approach to mental health which focuses on what works, is accessible to all, and yet still offers a wide choice to individuals. Overwhelmingly, they wanted to have someone to talk to. They found that compared to physical treatments such as medication and ECT, 88 per cent of their sample said they found 'talking treatments', far more helpful.

However, it must be said that the success of talking therapies does depend very much on the therapist, their professional orientation, and the relationship with the client. In 1992 Dee carried out a small research project based on 25 women and, sadly, she found that the majority of the women she spoke to had not had positive experiences of counselling, group therapy and psychotherapy.

The right relationship between therapist and client must be established from the outset, and if you feel that a therapist isn't listening to what you have to say, or appears averse to discussing your self-harm, it is vital that you discuss the problem with them and, if necessary, ask to change to a different person who will help you give voice to your inner life.

> I've found both doctors and psychiatrists very indifferent and unsympathetic. Although my therapist is understanding, even she finds it very difficult to tolerate and doesn't really like me telling her what I've done or what I felt like doing.
>
> Chrissie

The theoretical orientation of a therapist determines the process of the therapy and also the meaning that is given to your self-harm. A selection of those therapies most commonly used today are described in the following sections.

Behavioural Interventions

Some women who self-harm are referred to a behaviour therapist (BT) or a Community Psychiatric Nurse (CPN) for help with behavioural techniques aimed at trying to stop the acts of self-harm. Behavioural techniques are based on the idea that only behaviour that leads to reward is repeated. Hence they try and establish what rewards are gained from a particular behaviour. Change is brought about either by altering the way those rewards are obtained or by preventing those rewards from being accessed by that behaviour. Such techniques, however, aim to stop the behaviour without dealing with the real cause.

Unfortunately there are behaviour therapists who employ very simplistic approaches to complex problems. One such technique is 'thought stopping' which involves telling yourself to stop, and to imagine a STOP sign whenever the urge to self-harm begins to build up. When used alone and without any other form of empathetic understanding of what may be the root of the feelings leading to self-harm, such simplistic interventions do little to gain trust, respect and credibility for the behavioural method of treatment being used. Some women also find these techniques offensive.

The programme you are more likely to be offered is one in which you will be expected to look at the factors that lead up to the need to self-harm (the antecedents) and the consequences after you have self-harmed. You can then try and change the sequence of events that cause you to injure yourself. In order to do this you have to keep a very detailed diary to record all your thoughts, feelings and behaviours up to, during and after an episode of self-harm. Thus a personal cycle of behaviour can be derived and you will be able to identify points in the cycle where interventions can be made. An example of such a cycle is shown opposite.

Looking at Lucy's cycle, there are several places where a behaviour therapist might suggest an intervention. These might include working on ways to stop the cycle of negative thinking by for example (1) arranging to phone someone when she begins to think like this; or (2) trying alternative methods of reducing tension; or (3) by ensuring she is not alone or is unable to buy the things she needs to self-harm. This is only the most basic of examples, to give you an idea how a behavioural programme might work.

Behavioural approaches to self-harm can foster hostile and punitive attitudes in the professionals overseeing them by emphasising control and power over the behaviour of others. This is not a necessary feature of such approaches but can be an unfortunate 'by product'.

Complex forms of behaviour therapy can help change patterns of self-harm but they do not address how it started or what it means. If there is a traumatic event at the root of the distress, this is unlikely to be addressed. However, learning new patterns of behaviour may be useful and practical for some women who self-harm.

Example – Lucy's Cycle

Any occurrence that made her
feel rejected

↓

(1) Feeling unlovable as if she is
unwanted
feeling hurt and angry and
remembering all the other
people and times when she
has felt this way

↓ ↑

(2)   Tension becomes unbearable

↓

Need to reduce this tension

↓

Reinforces beliefs → Knows that in the past cutting
that cutting works   has helped

↑   ↓

Feelings of calm

↑   ↓

Self-harm

↑

Making sure she
is alone

←

(3) Going out and   Finding reasons to prevent herself
buying new razors   from cutting meanwhile
and gauze   becoming unable to think of much
                                  other than the need to self-harm

Sometimes it is not important for an individual to discuss or process their traumatic material, but it is very important to learn how to avoid harming themselves. If that is the case for you then this form of intervention may be exactly what you are looking for. Other women have stated that this kind of work helps for some time but the relief often seems to be temporary or self-harm is 'replaced' by other behaviour such as an eating disorder or a problem with alcohol. They say that it was only dealing with the original trauma that led to a genuine reduction in their level of distress.

Trauma-Focused Therapy

Some therapists, while not ignoring the self-harming behaviour itself, believe that if the trauma is worked through and integrated into the woman's experience, then she will not feel the need to self-harm. This type of approach provides a respectful, validating, positive and supportive relationship. The woman is not seen as 'ill' but as a person whose life has been shaped by having to adapt to an unbearably distressing event.

> My counsellor has never allowed me to manipulate her which is vital. She's made it quite clear she disapproves of what I do but not of me as a person.
>
> Chrissie

The aim of therapy is to help the woman approach thoughts and feelings associated with the trauma she experienced that she has spent much of her life avoiding, often engaging in severe acts of self-harm in order to do so. If you are going to undertake this work it is important that you feel safe within the relationship with your therapist and also have some degree of support from friends or family as you will have to face the many difficult and painful feelings that you have had to block out over the years. The aim of doing this is so that you can resolve your previous traumatic experiences, and regain a sense of control over your emotions without resort to self-harm or any other tension-reducing behaviour. Trauma-focused therapy assumes that the more you know of your trauma and your response to it, the more readily you can integrate it into your sense of self. Once you have acknowledged and assimilated it there will no longer be this area of psychic terror that has be avoided at all costs in order to survive.[6]

Specific Therapy for Women Who Self-Harm (Bristol Model)[7]

This therapy has many features in common with trauma-focused therapy but the issue of self-harm is much more prominent and explicit. The starting point is that self-harm 'is instrumental: it serves important psychological functions'.[8] In this approach the therapist does not 'insist, require or ask' a woman to stop injuring herself. However, the therapist must be committed to understanding the meaning this behaviour has for her client and use this to help the client understand and express the feelings behind the behaviour. In doing so, new ways of coping can be found. The therapist must also recognise and comprehend any uncomfortable feelings or reactions she herself may have in response to her client's self-harm, as it is argued that 'the prejudices, beliefs and idealistic opinions of the therapist influence the outcome more strongly than the techniques applied'.[9] If you were to take part in this form of therapy, while not asking you to stop self-harming, the therapist would try to help you understand and express the feelings behind the behaviour and examine alternative ways of coping.

As self-harm is seen as a means of coping with painful experience and difficulty, the main focus of the work is an exploration of these underlying events. The therapy aims to make the link between the self-harming behaviour and the generating trauma/s. The social and political context in which you live and the role that this plays in your experience, is also acknowledged by the therapist and used in helping you understand your behaviour.

You are helped to make connections between things which have happened to you and the feelings associated with those events. It is believed that 'once the full agony has become understood to the individual as "This is how I feel", "This happened to me" or "This is part of myself", it becomes harder to self-injure'.[10]

Dialectical Behaviour Therapy (DBT)

DBT is a form of therapy devised by Marsha Linehan for people who are suffering from borderline personality disorder (BPD), a diagnosis often given to women who self-harm. Marsha Linehan's theory is that women who are given such a diagnosis have a biological disposition to finding it difficult to manage their emotions. If women with this biological disposition experience what Marsha calls an 'invalidating environment' within which they have inappropriate, erratic or insensitive responses to their thoughts, beliefs, feelings and sensations, they will find it very difficult to regulate the way they react.

DBT appears to be very specific about the order in which treatment targets are set and addressed. The major aims are to stop self-injuring and life-threatening behaviours, remove any blocks to therapy, and then change behaviours that make it impossible for a woman to achieve a reasonable quality of life. You will only be accepted into this therapy programme if you agree to work on stopping self-harming behaviour; however most DBT therapists do recognise how difficult this is for people to commit to after years of self-harm. You will be taught coping skills to use at times of stress and distress and the task of the individual therapist is to help you to adopt different approaches to dealing with moments of emotional crisis.

Individual therapy takes place once a week and you will also be given the therapist's telephone number so that you can make contact between sessions should a crisis occur. The therapist works to establish a strong positive interpersonal relationship with you from the start. As in other forms of therapy, the value of a genuine, accepting, caring relationship is fully recognised. Initially, the main purpose of your sessions is to examine any problematic event in detail and help you to find alternative solutions (similar to the behavioural work described above).

You will also attend a weekly group which is for the purpose of skills training. You can then use these skills to deal with problematic situations and improve your quality of life. The point-by-point programme involves such ideas as: crisis surviving strategies, for example, distraction, self-soothing, mindfulness, improving the moment; and reducing vulnerability to negative emotions by balancing your life, treating physical illness, eating properly, avoiding mood-altering drugs, sleeping enough, getting exercise; and building self-esteem by trying to do one thing each day to make yourself feel competent and in control. Another adult who is close to you is also taught skills so they can also coach you in times of acute crisis.

Initially the emphasis in both the group work and the individual therapy is on skills training. After you feel more able to control and deal with emotional crises without resort to self-harm, work in individual sessions focuses more on exploring the traumas in your life. During this time, if you have completed the skills training group, you can join a support group.

Research has indicated good results for women who have completed this programme as compared to more conventional treatments involving drugs or more non-specific psychotherapies. Many women say that they have found this multi-level approach very useful – they have experienced a great deal of help and support from being with other members of the group and have made considerable progress in dealing with many aspects of their lives in addition to stopping self-harm. However, some women say that they could not cope with the initial imperative to cease self-harming and others did not even begin the programme because they felt they would be too controlled by the regime of the therapy. Sadly, some women also described feeling unable to undertake the programme as they did not have anyone close enough to them to help them with the coaching, which is unfortunate, as not having such a person in your life certainly does not preclude you from taking part in this therapy.

On the whole, women who have managed to complete the programme describe feeling empowered, very much more in control of their lives, and enjoying a far better quality of life.

> I never thought I'd stick it at first – it all seemed so structured but I was desperate and it seemed my last hope. I was terrified of the group. I thought I'd have to tell everyone all about myself but it wasn't like that. I made some good friends in the group and they understood what I felt as they had been through it too. I had no supporter at first but there was another woman in the group who also had no supporter and so we decided to support each other. It was not easy but it was so worth it. I use the skills in some way almost everyday. In the last year I have only self-harmed twice.
>
> Sue

Family Therapy

Given that difficulties in relationships are so often cited as the trigger in the self-harming episodes researched, it seems odd that so little attention is given to a more systemic approach to treatment which involves those who form part of the woman's social circle.

> I felt as though I needed to hide how I felt from my mum, so I never cried or showed any emotions in front of her...I still desperately wanted a mother and latched on to women who I thought were good mothers – finding it very painful when it ended or I got pushed away because I demanded too much.
>
> Stacey

When women self-harm, it is almost always in private and often great effort will be made to protect the family from the impact of their feelings and behaviour, particularly if children are involved. However, it is likely that families *are* affected, at the very least indirectly, by the woman's distress and may have some awareness regarding how they cope with it.

If you feel that this may be relevant to your situation, family therapy can help the individual members of your family to become more sensitive to the situation and perhaps intervene in ways that are more helpful to you. Additionally, you may be very concerned that you are passing on 'bad habits' to your children. This may involve bottling up feelings; even though you know it is best to voice your inner emotions, it is hard for children to do so when their mother so clearly has trouble expressing hers. This can lead to the misconception that feelings are scary, frightening, and should be avoided. It can be reassuring to work together with your partner and children (if you have them) even if you are engaged in a more intensive form of individual treatment. You can use this forum to try out new skills you have learned, to reassure your children in particular that you are okay and you can manage your feelings; to tell your story to people who are important to you or to make more specific requests for help from the people who value and support you.

Being able to talk things through with your family also provides a space for others to raise their concerns with you. This might include their fear for you, their desire that things were better, their confusion about what to do or just to let you know how much they are already aware of. It is not uncommon for children to be much more aware of a parent's self-harm than the parent ever thought. They can also think the situation is much more serious. For example, the difference between cuts to harm and cuts to kill will almost certainly be lost on small children and only very experienced partners or care-givers will have learnt this distinction.

Choosing a Therapist

When you are looking for a therapist, you do not necessarily need to find someone who specialises in working with women who self-harm. The most important factor is that you find someone you feel you can get on with, who seems to understand you; someone you can grow to trust. The relationship that develops between you has repeatedly been shown to be the most important factor in bringing about change, regardless of the kind of talking therapy that is offered.

> I want someone who I can talk to, who treats me like a real person and makes me feel that I'm cared about. I want help to understand myself and feel in control of my life. I want to stop hurting myself, to learn other ways of coping. I don't want to be made to feel ashamed of myself anymore, ashamed of what I do to mentally survive.
>
> Lucy

Nevertheless you may feel that certain approaches are more suited to you and your circumstances. So if you decide you prefer one form of therapy to another, you can raise this with your GP when you discuss the help you want.

When you go for therapy, particularly if you have been on a waiting list for a long time, it often feels as if you have little or no choice and you have to accept whoever you get. However, if you do not feel comfortable or safe with your therapist, whatever the method of therapy, it is unlikely you will develop a trusting relationship through which you can explore your feelings. Not all therapists can provide the right environment within a therapeutic relationship. Michelle Webster has written about emotional abuse in therapy.[12] She describes this as 'not being there emotionally' for the client. If you feel your therapist is 'not there for you', and you continue in this therapeutic relationship, your situation is unlikely to improve. At worse the therapy will harm you even more.[13]

It is vital that you feel able to talk about your self-harming behaviour. Sometimes the inhibitions may not come from you but from the professional who feels anxious about the topic and conveys a strong non-verbal message to you that they don't want to talk about it.

> I was about 23 when I first started doing it. The only people who knew I did it were my husband and a CPN, who, believe me, *never ever* let me talk about it.
> Rowena

You *do* need to tell your therapist that you self-harm. If they cannot manage or deal with it, better to find out before you start rather than later. If you decide not to tell them, any discussions about past traumatic events may trigger self-harming episodes, because the pace of the therapy may be too rapid for you to manage.

Check that the person you are going to work with has an understanding of the issue that fits with your own understanding, or that you feel comfortable with.

The therapist I've had over this past year (as part of the college I was attending) was very good. She's never ignored what I do...it's OK for me to discuss what I do...

Chris

You may need to try more than one therapist before you meet one you feel at ease with. The most important characteristic to look for is someone who shows you empathy. Research has shown that empathy, warmth, genuineness and unconditional positive regard of the helper provide some of the most important ingredients to recovery work.[14] Professional training and expertise does not necessarily guarantee that a therapist will have these qualities.

Most people in therapy see their therapist as a very important person in their lives. Therefore it is not surprising that some women who find it very difficult to communicate their needs in any other way could use self-harm as a means of enlisting their therapist's sympathy, help and support.

There's definitely a relationship between inflicting wounds on myself and gaining attention from specific people, usually mother figures. In this respect my injuries are used as a way of manipulating people – it only works half the time.

Chris

If, however, you only feel that your therapist gives you care and attention when you self-harm, then you should think of looking for another, as the therapeutic relationship is clearly not giving you what you need.

Many women who are not in a good therapeutic relationship and feel uncomfortable with their therapist feel they are misjudging the situation and that the help they are being offered is good enough – they disqualify their own feelings of disquiet. Although it is really difficult to do so, try and discuss your concerns with your therapist. If you feel that they are basically honest and really trying to help you, and are taking responsibility for their own limitations, you may decide to stick with them and work through the difficulties. However, if they are hiding behind their professional role, insinuating that it is 'your fault' and making comments that suggest they are disconnected from how you are feeling, seriously consider whether this is helping you.

> I decided I needed help and started to see various psychotherapists. They were either not aware of my problem with self-harm or refused to deal with it. At the end of that time I felt very alone and my problem escalated. One therapist just couldn't deal with my problems with self-harm so she stopped seeing me – just like that. I was distraught. My self-harm became much worse for a time.
>
> Dee

There is a lot of evidence to show that talking treatments are not offered to some groups of clients as often as others – black men and women, for example, are not referred as often as their white counterparts.[15] Sometimes women who self-harm can be seen as 'too disturbed' for talking therapies, or you may find that what the therapist wants to discuss is not what you want to discuss. This frequently happens to lesbians, for example, where a therapist focuses on their sexual orientation and does not discuss the issue of self-harm.

Talking with other women who self-harm and comparing your experiences can give you the courage to complain if the treatment you are receiving really isn't helping you, or worse, is positively harming you. Also, therapy only takes place over a set time each week, and you may need support at other times. You might find it helpful to consider getting such support by joining to a self help group, or by phoning a help-line specifically run for women who self-harm by women who currently self-harm or who have done so in the past. Self-harm can be a very lonely experience, but by meeting or speaking to other women who are going through the same thing, you can begin to find solace and real understanding.

Chapter 5
Self-Help

Self-help – sharing experiences, knowledge and feelings with other women – can be an important part of your endeavour to stop self-harming. Self-help is when women work together and support each other, taking positive action to change our lives. This can be very empowering, giving us a feeling of control over our lives, making us feel understood, helping us to receive care and attention from others. At the same time we can enjoy the experience of being able to give similar care to others.

Self-Help Groups

Given the distress and dissatisfaction that many women experience with conventional treatments and public services, it is no wonder that a large number turn to self-help groups to find the help and understanding they crave. For some women, a self-help group alone can be an effective form of support, but for most, the ideal situation is a combination of self-help alongside more conventional therapy. Being in such a group and thus increasing your support also makes it less likely that you will be so vulnerable to a bad therapeutic experience.

Unfortunately self help groups, alternative and complementary therapies often have to be funded by the clients themselves. All too often they are also, along with voluntary sector provision, filling the gaps in the service provided by the health authority.

There are both advantages and disadvantages to belonging to a self-help group and you will need to decide if this approach will benefit your particular situation. For example, though self-help groups are very positive and encouraging in the help that they can offer someone who self-harms, they are often not able to provide appropriate care for someone who feels desperate or suicidal.

> I tried to kill myself. Before I moved to this hostel I was living rough for 12 days then the social worker brought me here...I am now seeing someone who is trying to sort out my problem.
>
> Sharon B

Someone who is suicidal needs a different kind of care. If you feel like this, you should look for support from a specially trained individual who deals frequently with people in your situation and who has a thorough understanding of the issues involved.

You will need a certain degree of stability in your life if you are to get the most out of a self-help group. You will need physical stability – for example, it is hard to talk about your distress if you don't even know where you are going to sleep. You will also need a certain degree of emotional stability, as you may find it too distressing to listen to other women's issues.

Nevertheless self-help groups do offer a great deal to most women who self-harm. The range of support usually includes the following:

- telephone support
- weekly meetings
- group support from other women who self-harm
- counselling
- a safe haven for self-expression
- newsletters, worksheets and poetry
- advocates for trips to A & E
- advice about rights
- understanding
- new friends

Gerry Cooney of MIND says, 'People need asylum in the true sense of the word.' Self-help groups can offer this kind of asylum. At the first National Conference on Self-harm in September 1989 several speakers stressed the need for an accepting and caring, rather than rejecting reaction to self-harm. There was a call for access to services such as counselling, groupwork and a 24-hour telephone helpline.[1]

If no self-help group exists in your area, you might think about setting one up yourself. Setting up and running a self-help group has its problems and pitfalls. Funding is one of the most pervasive problems suffered by these groups; it costs money even just to run the group. Additionally, those who could provide funding are sometimes resistent to the idea because they do not believe that self-help is a real alternative or a benefit to women who self-harm. You may need to argue your case, which can be frustrating and even daunting at times.

It is a good idea to make some ground rules at the outset regarding turn taking, confidentiality and how to make sure that you pay attention to your own and other's safety. When we have unmet needs and are in pain, we sometimes avoid addresing this by helping others instead. We can be very helpful, caring and sensitive to others, but do nothing to help ourselves; we can become compulsive carers while still struggling to deal with our own pain. The issue of whether there is a set group leader or facilitator, or whether the role of facilitator should be rotated amongst group members needs to be decided. Dealing with other women who are suffering a great deal of distress can be exhausting and must be handled delicately. The facilitator should be able to carefully calm down anyone who becomes really upset and distressed. She also needs to have the ability to lead meetings in such a way that all members can have some kind of input. All sorts of people self-harm, some extremely quiet, some aggressive; some well-spoken, some uncommunicative; but all have the right to help and support. Women from all walks of life and with a variety of problems may join and each deserves the same treatment. If it is decided that the group will be facilitated by one specific person, that need not necessarily be another woman who self-harms. Some women may feel inhibited if the facilitator does not self-harm as they may assume that that person cannot possibly understand how it must feel. Other women say they feel safer if the facilitator does not self-harm, because they will be able to hear and contain people's feelings without becoming too affected themselves. But the most important characteristic the facilitator should possess, whether they self-harm or not, is the ability to remain calm and non-judgemental in any given situation, and empathetic to the needs of each member of the group.

There are various ways in which we all typically interact and these patterns can sometimes be replicated within a self-help group. Women generally have a tendency to put other people's needs before our own. This can be just as true when we are in all female groups. It may be difficult for you to take your turn to get help and support; you may find you are being the strong one and listening to everyone else. This can make you feel better for a while but later on, you might begin to feel lonely and isolated. Alternatively, you may find that you are talking about yourself all the time and can't seem to stop. You might feel you have made yourself too vulnerable and rather than feeling better about yourself, feel angry for saying too much.

Sometimes self-help groups unintentionally encourage women to self-harm, or to try methods of harming they have not previously used. Clearly this is not the purpose of the group, but you should be alert to the possibility that it can happen.

> Someone at a meeting told me how they had achieved horrific burns to their arms and I knew that I had to try it. I'm ashamed to admit that I was very pleased with the resulting burns. It sounds so sick, saying it like that now but I really was that suggestible when I self-harmed.
>
> Dee

To avoid this situation, facilitators, and group members, need to be aware of the dynamics within the group, particularly any dynamics that are related to conflict.

One of the most positive aspects of self-help groups, is the opportunity to meet other women who share the same problem and with whom you can talk freely about your self-harm.

> When things were very bad, I felt out of control, and the self-harming made me feel very alone. So it was very comforting to find other women who self-harm that I could meet with and talk to. They knew how I felt and they didn't look disgusted when I talked about all the things I'd done to myself.
>
> Dee

They allowed me to discuss my problems freely without worrying about being sectioned. I knew that everything I said stayed within the group. It wasn't written down and chucked back at me later. I felt safe, I could tell the others anything without shocking them, they knew how bad things could be.

Janet

Professionals; CPNs, doctors, and psychologists, generally seem happy to recommend self-help groups to their clients. Such recommendations often provide most of the women who attend these groups, whereas advertising does little to draw people in.[2] If they remain focused and positive, self-help groups not only offer a great deal of support, but can also provide lasting friendships.

Check List Setting Up Self-Help Groups

To begin a group there are several factors you should consider:

1. Do you have an appropriate meeting place – somewhere that is quiet and comfortable, offering privacy, which you can use on a regular basis? Does it have kitchen and toilet facilities? Can anyone use it, including disabled members?
2. Do you have funding? Apply for grants, talk to the local mental health team or the Council. Can you raise money yourselves?
3. Do you have links with the local community including psychiatrists, doctors, CPNs? Can you advertise your group?
4. Do you have a suitable facilitator who can remain impartial when things get tough, who can talk and listen where appropriate? Do you want to rotate the facilitator? Will each group member feel able to do this?

5. Have you got time to organise things so that meetings have some sort of structure? Can you get suitable information for your group and organise talks about First Aid and other relevant issues?

6. Lastly, can you cope with even the most horrible forms of self-harm – especially when you feel bad yourself? Can you remain supportive and caring when really you feel angry and fed up? Will you be able to manage someone who is very ill, whose distress may even frighten you. Consider how you will react.

If you have decided to set up a self-help group, but it does not seem to be getting off the ground as quickly as you would like, remember it can often take a long time for things to start coming together. It is important to meet regularly even if there are only one or two of you. Once people start to hear about the group, other women will come along.

Telephone Lines

If you are very isolated geographically, or you are too physically ill, attending a self-help group is not a viable option. Or you may not feel ready for a group for what ever reason. However, there are other resources, such as telephone counselling which can be a useful means of support. In the main, such lines are usually run by other women who self-harm. Telephone lines are especially helpful in a crisis because they are there at the moment when you need to talk. This may, in turn, actually stop you from hurting yourself.

Many of us find it hard to talk about our feelings face to face; it can sometimes be easier to talk about them when you don't have the non-verbal cues of your listener to consider. You can also end your call whenever you want, which gives you maximum control. In addition, telephone lines also reach a wider audience than self-help groups. Some provide support for caregivers, friends, and family members of women who self-harm, and some are also used by professionals.

One of the major weaknesses of most existing telephone lines is that many are only available at certain times of the day. To be really beneficial, the line should be available 24 hours a day, every day of the year.

> Several times I rang the Samaritans in an effort to stop harming when really a counsellor who dealt only with self-harm would have been more able to help. The Samaritans were very kind but what could they say?
>
> Dee

When you are in a crisis, it can add to your distress if you try to get help and do not seem to be able to get any. The lack of an answer can seem like a rejection, and can almost become some form of justification to self-harm – a kind of Russian roulette approach to whether or not you self-harm. You may begin to feel your self-harm is controlling you, and that you are powerless to stop it on your own.

> I tried to ring once, but no one answered so I self-harmed anyway.
>
> Janet

If you find yourself in this situation, do try other helplines, as simply talking to someone may ease your tension and provide enough relief until you do manage to get through to a specialist in self-harm.

Newsletters

Another way of breaking down the isolation of self-harm is through newsletters. You can use them to communicate how you feel by writing and many women could also benefit from what you have written as you may have put into words how they are feeling. Newsletters often have a very wide circulation. They can be read anywhere, any time, and can reach anyone, however remote that person feels they might be. Newsletters publish articles, letters, poems, reviews, pen-pal contacts, artwork and educational pieces as well as listing details of services available to you and those who are closely involved in your life.

Newsletters do require some funding but are not that expensive to run, and can relay vital information about self-harm to anyone who wishes to read it. Women who self-harm can remain anonymous whilst contributing, so they can get help without worrying about people's reactions. We all feel much safer expressing ourselves if we feel we can do so in a place where we know we will be free from judgement and criticism, where there are no constraints on self-expression. Those women who prefer to keep their self-harm a secret from others can continue to do so and those who find face-to-face support traumatic, for whatever reason, can also benefit from the anonymity newsletters offer.

For those with access to the Internet, there is a newsletter for people who self-harm on **http.//crystal palace.net/~llama/psych/injury.html**. It includes a message board and a chat room as well as general information on self-harm. Like telephone lines it provides an immediate outlet for your feelings and the chance to connect with others who self-harm.

There are certain difficulties associated with newsletters. Firstly, it is hard to advertise such a newsletter which means a great many women remain completely unaware of its existence; and secondly, however well run it is, there is bound to be a subscription fee to cover running costs. This may mean there are women who would like to receive it, but cannot afford it.

When setting up a newsletter, it is important to remember to make a provision for people who cannot pay subscription by adding the cost of free subscriptions to the total price charged for those who can pay. It does play an important role in providing help and support for those who are fighting to live without self-harm.

Taking Care of Yourself

Learning how to care for yourself is an essential survival skill. If you do self-harm it is very important that you look after your injuries. You should learn to assess whether or not your injuries need medical attention, because if you do not get appropriate medical care, you may become seriously ill. If cuts or burns are not properly treated, for example, they can lead to septicaemia (blood poisoning). If you ingest poisons, even small amounts can lead to death in certain circumstances. Women have told us that they sometimes know they need medical help, but do not get it, as their past experiences have been so aversive. If you are worried about going to the Accident and Emergency Department when you have self-harmed, try and ask someone to go with you. It is better if you make this arrangement before you need their help, and discuss it with them, so that they feel able to talk for you when confronted by the staff. Remember you may be in shock and find it difficult to speak out in the way that you normally would. The organisation Survivors Speak Out suggests using a crisis card. This is a card which draws attention to your particular difficulties and recommends ways of helping you when you are so distressed you cannot speak for yourself.[3]

Despite being able to harm yourself without feeling pain, by the time you arrive at hospital you may well feel a great deal. You should feel able to ask for pain relief if you need it, especially if you are going to have stitches. Pain relief is rarely offered. Some women say it is a difficult thing to ask for as they feel that they are to blame for their own pain. Nevertheless you have a right to be free of pain however it was caused. Other women do not want pain relief – they see the pain as part of their punishment, or the physical pain distracts from, and is preferable to, their psychological torment.

Once in hospital, unless you are a danger to yourself or others, you cannot forcefully be detained under the Mental Health Act. You are free to leave whenever you want to. However you may be at risk of being sectioned if the staff feel you will self-harm again very soon, or if your visit is one of a series. You may want to discuss this with someone you trust so that, should the need arise, this person can act as an advocate for you.

If your injuries do not require professional medical treatment, they do still need first aid. Also looking after yourself and keeping yourself healthy is a way of nurturing yourself. The following are some basic tips that can help you judge whether you need medical help, and if not how to care for your own injuries.

Cuts

Is the cut bleeding profusely? Is there a spurt? If so it may be an arterial spurt. Either way you should go straight to hospital for immediate attention. However, if you cannot or will not go, there are a few measures which you can take to minimise the damage.

1. Stop the bleeding by putting direct pressure on to the wound. Elevate the damaged area if at all possible whilst applying pressure as this will slow the bleeding. Do not apply a tourniquet as this is likely to cause further damage.
2. Stitches may be necessary. However, if you refuse to go to hospital, once the bleeding slows down, clean

the wound and use Steri-strips (otherwise known as butterfly strips) to hold the edges of the wound together.

3. Whether they are deep or minor wounds they need to be kept clean. Spray with an antiseptic spray or use an antiseptic wipe. Antiseptic cream from a tube is not as useful as this can spread germs. Dress even the most minor wounds to lessen the chances of infection setting in.

4. Never use dirty or old razors when you cut yourself and never use dirty bits of glass that you pick up from the street or garden.

Burns

A burn is almost always very dangerous and larger burns certainly need medical attention. Remember that the fluid loss from a large burn can be very serious and there is a constant risk of infection. Cool the burnt area immediately in running cold water, leaving it under the water for at least ten minutes, as this can radically reduce the damage. If possible, wrap the burn loosely in clingfilm and seek medical attention as quickly as you can. If the burn has only blistered don't touch it, but cover it with a sterile dressing. Do not burst any blisters that may form as this just opens the way for infection to occur. When you are buying dressings for burns you need to ask for a specialist burn dressing which is covered in a jelly to stop it from sticking to the wound.

Poisons

If you ingest poison please do try to ask for help. Seeking medical attention is very important and delay can often prove fatal. This is because some drugs and chemicals, although excreted by the body, can cause respiratory suppression or be absorbed into the bloodstream and cause liver failure. Some poisons accumulate in the body suppression or be absorbed into the bloodstream and cause liver failure. Some poisons accumulate in the body and eventually even a small quantity that seems non-lethal can kill you.

Signs of Septicemia (Blood Poisoning)

Try not to be complacent about your wounds, never let them become infected. Never be afraid of asking for help!

Always be alert and look out for signs of blood poisoning. This can be very serious, even life-threatening, and is especially common with burns. Signs to look out for are fever, abscesses, rashes and chills. Does your wound throb and is it hot? If you think the answer is yes, please seek immediate medical attention.

Reducing and Repairing the Harm

Many women who self-harm are never very far from the things they use to injure themselves. You can tell you are beginning to cope in a different way when you can be further and further away from the things you have used in the past. One protective measure you can take if you tend to cut or burn yourself is to keep your own first aid kit alongside the equipment with which you harm yourself. This is all part of your attempt to care for yourself at the basic level. For example you may keep a small, clean tin with you at all times which contains:

- Steri-strips
- Antiseptic wipes
- Sterile dressings

This enables you to repair any damage you might do to your body. Including things to help you heal is an important step in learning to live more distantly from your self-harm, and taking care of yourself is an essential part of your recovery.

Chapter 6
Disrupting Self-Harm Patterns

> I don't want to do it but I don't know what else to do
> instead
>
> Lisa (from her diary)

There is a great deal of evidence that self-harm is part of a learned pattern of coping and that it can become addictive.[1] You can become used to always feeling keyed up, waiting for something to happen. You can become resigned to self-harm going on endlessly. Learning to change how you cope with overwhelming feelings is not easy. Like any other form of change, the motivation has to come from you. This motivation can sometimes be very hard to sustain, because giving up a coping strategy takes a long time. Unfortunately there is no magical 'cure'.

> I feel so alone in my pain, alone in my fear. I built a self-harm wall around me originally as self-protection, but it has now become my jailer, preventing anyone getting in to help me. I want to remove the wall but am trapped inside, it's been there for so long, it is so thick, so high. I want someone to come and break down the

wall and get me out but even then I am not sure that I could step out. It is so lonely in here but I know no other world, fear keeps me in here.

Cathy

To give up what has helped you survive for so long is very difficult. You will need time to change. It will be an emotionally painful process and should be taken slowly. Every day you survive without self-harming is an achievement. Self-harm may have helped get you this far but it is unlikely to get you beyond your pain and your past. Some women describe it as feeling like a death sentence hanging over them. They also recognise the pain that their self-harm causes to those who love and care for them and can feel very guilty about this.

Some women say they think that they will never be able to stop, but many do. There will have been times in your own life when you wanted to self-harm but didn't, you *did* stop. Think more about those times and try to recall what stopped you. You may also remember a period when you didn't self-harm at all, or the episodes were much less frequent. What was different about that time in your life? The exceptions to your pattern of self-harming give you clues as to what you need in order to break your self-harming cycle. If you decide you want to stop, this will help you think about what will enable you to do so. It is likely that you will need help to support you through this process. That help could come from statutory or voluntary agencies, from an individual or from a group, or from both.

Disrupting your pattern of self-harm is a process:

- you will need to get to know your own patterns, not only about when you do self-harm but also when you don't
- you will need to learn when you are most vulnerable to self-harm and what emotional states are likely to trigger this behaviour

- it will be important to identify and work through the original trauma and process the associated feelings while beginning to learn other ways of coping
- *feel* your feelings, communicate those emotions and meet your needs

Getting to Know Your Own Pattern – Recording

It can be useful to record when you self-harm. In this way you can detect any patterns associated with the passage of time. What is the longest you have been without self-harming? Do episodes seem to occur at the same time of day? Week? Month? Year? Is this time associated with other significant (often traumatic), events in your life? Is it related to your menstrual cycle? Seasons of the year? This can help you to identify times when you may be more vulnerable and more likely to hurt yourself. When you start to think of strategies for breaking old self-harming patterns, you can then build in this information into your plan.

Recording is also useful in that you can write down exactly what you are experiencing at the time when you are feeling it most intensely. Sometimes just the activity of writing everything in a stream of consciousness helps to avert the crisis. If you find writing too difficult, you could use audio tape instead – dictating machines are especially useful for this as you can turn them on and off easily. If you do harm yourself on occasion, you will then have a record of how you felt at the time, which is something you could go through and talk about with someone you trust who is committed to helping you stop.

Looking back over recordings may also help you identify certain triggers. What happened before you began to feel so bad? How long was the build up to the episode? If feeling angry with someone is likely to trigger an episode, it can be helpful to write how you feel very soon after the interaction rather than later on when the angry feeling has become turned in on yourself.

Some people find that writing doesn't make them feel any better and when they reread what they have written, it increases both their tension and the desire to hurt themselves. If this is the case for you, it may be better for you to post or give your written material to someone else for safe-keeping. Otherwise you may find you begin to use the material to facilitate rather than hinder your next episode of self-harm. Sometimes you can read material written for or by you regarding your self-harm which can put into words your feelings and help you to stop an episode occurring.

> I want to cut when I feel angry, lonely/alone, confused. I feel I have no right to my feelings. I feel disgusting and dirty. I don't know what else to do. I want to hurt. I deserve to be hurt.
>
> *(This was written during a therapy session and taken away)*
>
> Diary entry – I have just cut myself again...I am shaking like a leaf. I did it because I felt lonely and confused about the past. I thought of the piece of paper that I've got that says: 'I want to cut when I feel...'
>
> Lisa

Lisa had just learnt the technique and at first did not use it; she remembered what she had written *after* she had cut heself. Slowly, however, she did begin to read what she had written prior to cutting herself. Using this technique, along with exploring and expressing her feelings in therapy, Lisa stopped self-harming.

RECORD YOUR SUCCESSES AS WELL. What has helped you to avert an episode? You may be able to use the same strategy again in the future. What makes you feel better about yourself, or your life? Maybe you should make more time for these things and do them more regularly.

This can involve taking care of yourself in positive ways. By giving yourself treats regularly and not just when you feel bad about yourself or before you are going to do something hurtful, you may begin to feel fundamentally better about yourself.

Recognising the Feelings that Lead to Self-Harm

Some women have said that when they are trying to record what they feel, they have great difficulty in knowing what it is they are actually experiencing. They know they feel tense and distressed, or feel emotionally 'numb', 'cut off', or 'dead', but they cannot describe the actual emotion. This is not surprising as one of the most common factors in the lives of women who self-harm is that they have experienced a traumatic incident, or series of traumatic incidents, and the resulting difficult feelings were not acknowledged. Consequently those feelings were not validated, or worked through. Also many women who self-harm describe having tried to tell people at various times about their feelings and getting a negative response. Thus any emotion connected with the trauma, and any similar feelings, have subsequently been denied or pushed away. Eventually it becomes very difficult to know what these feelings are at all. They become a profusion of sentiments which cannot be expressed, and so are repressed; 'pushed out of your mind' leaving you feeling 'numb' or intensely distressed. Both states can ultimately result in self-harm.

If this is your experience, you will probably need someone to help you explore in detail, within a safe emotional space, the feelings you had and what triggered them. The person you are sharing this with will then be able to help you identify what those feelings were and express them more clearly. The person most likely to assist you is a therapist who is trained in doing this, but other people may also be able to help.

You can then begin to work out which feelings lead you to self-harm.

> I realise I have been pushing down a lot of pain, hurt and anger for a lifetime...My bulimia and cutting myself are ways of expressing and dealing with unbearable pain.
>
> Julie

Identifying and Working Through the Original Trauma

You need to believe that you *can* find other ways of expressing what is going on inside you. Marsha Linehan talks about realistic acceptance of your feelings as an important part of your recovery.[2] By this she means that you begin to accept your feelings as a valid response to your experiences; believing that you have a right to those feelings. In order to do this you will almost certainly need to psychologically revisit the original trauma and articulate what you felt at that time. It will also help you to understand what made the feelings associated with that trauma so unbearable for you and for the people who should have been able to hear your pain and respond to it appropriately.

Dusty Miller encourages women to see their self-harm as a re-enactment of earlier traumatic experiences that have not been articulated and processed by the individual except through the repetitive acts of self-harm.[3] She sees recognising and affirming the pain that you have felt and currently feel as essential. It is also important that this pain is recognised by other people in your life. Some women say that they have done this first with a therapist who they have begun to trust, and then with close friends and partners. Others have said that they started with their partner, or at a self-help group. It is an individual choice and depends who is in your life and the kind of relationship you have with them.

> This Christmas my panic attacks overwhelmed me and I did self-harm again. This time though I decided to talk to others and within a matter of days I'd managed to control my problem again.
>
> Dee

Expressing the pain you feel and having that pain really acknowledged by someone else, can help take away the immediate need to harm yourself.

> At first I really couldn't see that talking about feelings was going to do anything to take away this terrible need to cut myself. Eventually though when I really began to be able to share what I felt and it seemed to me that people really heard and understood me, the feelings did pass, not immediately but they did, they really did.
>
> Lucy

We all need to have our feelings validated, recognised and seen as normal responses to our experiences. Much of the benefit of 'good' therapy is permission-giving, validation and empowerment. You have a right to your feelings whatever they may be. You may need help to articulate them. You may need someone else to name them for you because for so long you have denied them, or have had your feelings denied by others. You may want confirmation that your feelings are appropriate given the situation.

Sometimes women who self-harm say that this can initially feel very strange as other people in their lives have not previously done this. If you have always been told, implicitly or explicitly, that you did not have a right to your feelings, then it is very hard to own them, let alone believe that you have the right to share them with others. You may have been made to believe that your normal natural responses are unacceptable or invalid, or that you are not entitled to feel certain emotions such as anger or aggression. The feelings you have been denied are the ones that you tend to direct against yourself. Therefore having your feelings validated by others, especially people who are important to you, is extremely important.

It is a strong positive step to practice saying how you feel, day to day, with those around you. You may also need to learn how to manage conflict better. Many women who self-harm find it difficult to get angry with friends or family and, rather than express their angry feelings, store them up. This can lead to explosions of anger that are disproportionate to the precipitating incident or can, if bottled up, lead to an episode of self-harm.

Emotional outbursts are part of your recovery. Learning and letting yourself express your feelings in words rather than self-harming actions is another crucial ingredient. You will also have to learn how to manage other people's reactions. They may not be used to you expressing your feelings, especially members of your family. Friends and supportive others may be shocked or taken aback when you begin to talk about how you feel. You may be too sensitive to begin with, but in time you will begin to learn how to calibrate your own emotional repertoire.

The first time I shouted at my partner it was a shock to both of us. He'd arranged something I didn't want to do, I was annoyed but usually when I felt like that I'd brood, just say nothing, hold it in. I'd expect him to notice and if he didn't I'd just get angrier and angrier and more and more tense until I cut. But this time it was so different, I actually shouted at him, and he shouted back and then we realised and we both just laughed and he hugged me. I actually shouted at him and he accepted my anger. It was amazing, I felt so free.

Lucy

Once you begin to look at and share your feelings of pain and distress, you begin to take charge of your own healing. However, it is very important you pace your recovery work. Pushing yourself too hard to remember everything can be overwhelming and produce extreme feelings of fear and loathing that you are unlikely to be able to process or manage. So you don't have to deal with everything at once, but with each issue or emotion as it arises. Some professionals who work with trauma feel that it is important for the client's recovery that the whole story is told. However, telling stories in part can be just as useful and may also be more manageable in the long term. Maybe that is why we remember in fragments. As we gain mastery over some fragments, more begin to emerge.

Feeling Your Feelings, Communicating Your Feelings and Getting Your Needs Met

Almost all women find it very difficult to communicate their needs to others. We are socialised not to express how we feel, nor to ask for what we want. We are more likely to meet the needs of others than consider what our requirements are. Self-harm is a way of meeting emotional need without seeming to put any demand on others. To stop self-harming, new ways of fulfilling those emotional demands have to be found.

Doing my diary made me realise that when I was lonely or wanted someone to comfort me or feel sorry for me I would hurt myself, usually on purpose but make it seem like an accident. I talked this through in the group and remembered when I was little I used to go to the school nurse with cuts and grazes and she would cuddle me and make me feel better. People always seem so much nicer to you if they think you've had an accident. It is hard at the moment as I am trying to tell the friends I've made in the group when I need them to be to be nice to me or I want to be comforted but it is so hard. I always think they will refuse or reject me but they haven't.

Sue

You have to allow yourself to experience your emotions in order to be able to identify what your needs are, and you have to do this without self-harming. Seeing self-harm as addictive can be helpful. This confirms the subjective experience you may have had that you need to self-harm and also suggests that stopping self-harming will be difficult and take time. We all develop addictions, both good and bad through repetition. Why some actions are repeated more than others often depends on the effect the action has – if those actions reduce stress and tension then it is more likely we will continue to use that action at other times of stress.

I'd taken drugs as a teenager. I understood about 'going cold turkey'. Describing it like that made me realise that it was something I had to go through. When it all seemed too much I'd tell myself, it'll pass just write down what you're feeling, try and make sense of it and eventually it would pass. I can't say at first it always stopped me cutting but the times when it did I felt really elated afterwards.

Steph

The way to break any addiction is to stop and go through 'withdrawal'. In the case of self-harm, to stop you have to allow yourself to go through the difficult and painful feelings that can seem so overwhelming. At these times it is hard to believe that feelings are transient and will go away. The belief that such feelings can only go away if you self-harm needs to be gently challenged. If you can delay an episode of self-harm even by an hour, this is a step towards gaining control. You can try to go longer each time. You may find you can ride the pain out the other side without harming yourself or that there are other harmless methods of reducing tension.

If you are working with a therapist you trust, you may need to spend some time at the beginning of your work specifically devising ways of managing the painful feelings that will be addressed. Articulating your feelings – aloud, in writing, through painting, drawing or movement – is all part of helping you to process traumatic material. Processing is like digestion. Taking something in, breaking it down into its constituent parts, keeping the good bits and getting rid of the bad bits. Our experiences, good or bad, contribute to our growth and development. Having the courage to begin processing the past is based on the hope that our lives will be better as a consequence. It opens up the possibility of change and difference for you.

In themselves, therapy sessions can often act as a trigger to overwhelming feelings. If this isn't addressed, you might begin to avoid therapy as a way of protecting yourself. The urge to self-harm often occurs outside of the therapeutic hour, and you will need a backup to help you in between sessions. There are some tactics that you can try that may help to prevent or delay self-harming. These methods are not an end in themselves but a means to an end; they are about giving yourself space and the chance to learn that you can feel your feelings without being overcome by them.

I still can't cry or show anger but I've come a long way...I'm trying to be just one person now, a spontaneous feeling person who doesn't need horrific secrets...

Stacey

Disrupting Your Self-Harm

1. Sharing Your Feelings

If there is someone you feel safe with and who you can talk to immediately about how you feel, do try and do so, even if it seems that you do not have the words to convey the intensity of your feelings. You could begin by describing where in your body you are feeling the tension. Describe the physical sensations you are experiencing. Describe what image you have of the emotion; is it an ache, a tear, a sharp object or a heavy block. Maybe talk about when you have felt this way before. If there is no one to talk to at that particular time, try writing down how you feel – you may want to do this in letter form to yourself or someone you are close to. Another useful technique is to answer a set of written questions regarding your feelings and the need to self-harm (you can set these yourself, or have others help you draw up a list). You may also feel more able to express your feelings through a different medium such as by drawing, painting or even modelling clay.

I know that one of the triggers to my self-harm was when I felt disgusting. I felt disgusting but couldn't say so. I wanted to look just as disgusting as I felt. I never hid my scars. Often I'd deliberately show them to repulse people. Burns were particularly effective for doing this. Jean (*a psychiatric nurse who greatly helped Sheena to begin to share her feelings and stop self-harming*) encouraged me to say just how disgusting I felt rather than harming myself. She never tried to say you're not repulsive. I think that would have made me want to hurt myself more. She'd ask me which parts of my body felt disgusting and we'd think together why. She really helped me understand that it was feeling him inside of me that made me feel so disgusting. When she wasn't on duty she encouraged me to draw how I felt about my body. Eventually I could say that what I needed was reassurance that I was not disgusting and that I needed someone to care for me and comfort me for who I am.

Sheena

2. Distraction

Some women find they can distract themselves enough to get through a crisis without self-harming. Some develop rituals that have to be followed before they 'allow' themselves to self-harm. Sometimes just by following these, the crisis itself passes and self-harm is averted. Paradoxically, 'allowing themselves the permission' to self-harm but following the rituals before they do so gives them the sense of control which helps them overcome the need they were feeling.

Other distractions from self-harming behaviours can involve:

- Finding an activity that is incompatible with harming yourself – this could involve contacting someone, going out, or taking care of yourself or someone else.
- Using relaxation techniques – you can get various tapes that can take you through the process of making you feel relaxed. Regular relaxation through meditation, yoga, or tai chi, for example, will, over time, make radical changes to your biochemistry but in a crisis (unless you have already mastered the techniques and been using them regularly) they are unlikely to make any appreciable difference.

These may work sometimes and not others. If this happens, it is important that you don't drop the distracter as useless – it just didn't work for you on that occasion. Because different feelings can trigger self-harming episodes, it makes sense that different strategies are going to be needed at different times.

When I began working with my therapist I was so surprised that she really seemed to want to hear what I felt. It was only then that I really realised that I didn't actually know what I felt, just that whatever it was made me feel so bad...even when we had begun to be able to talk about my feelings it didn't stop the urges to cut. Eventually I found I could stop myself by driving up onto the moors in the car and stopping at a quiet place. There I could just scream, and I would scream and scream and then I began to be able to cry. I had not cried since I was a child. The combination of the need to concentrate to drive and the permission to scream and scream when I got there was what helped me.

Debbie

3. Substitution

Substituting one form of self-harm for another is very common. Unfortunately the substitutes that give the same level of relief are often at least as harmful as the form of self-harm they replace. Many women harm themselves in a number of ways and at times one form of harm is more prominent than others. Tyler would spend days eating nothing and drinking only diet coke. She would then begin to eat again but misuse prescribed drugs so she was sedated all day long. At other times she would cut herself or burn herself with cigarette ends, but eat normally and be off most of her medication. This is not an uncommon pattern.

I began to cut at work...the minute cuts began to heal I'd pick them to make them bleed more. At this time my eating habits were very peculiar. I swung from periods of starvation to periods of bingeing...At one point I tried laxatives...I also had problems with panic attacks.

Dee

Crying – no way. Blades – yes. Booze – yes. Pills – yes.
Lisa

Some women do find that when they start to address their innermost feelings, they can avert an episode of self-harm by using a less dangerous way of hurting themselves. These can include methods such as squeezing ice cubes or stretching a rubber band and letting it spring back to hit you. Both of these are less harmful than most usual methods, but they often do not produce enough of a sensation to be a good alternative. They are temporary measures until you find other ways of coping with your feelings. Other women have found that exercise is a good way of releasing emotional tension. Some women find that exercise which involves releasing pent up aggression is a good substitute. Squash for example is particularly useful if you are feeling tense and angry as you can hit the ball hard against the wall, and shout and scream in a socially acceptable situation. You don't even need to play a game against someone. Obviously some sports are more readily available than others but with local sports and leisure centres growing up all over the country, a variety of sports are becoming more accessible.

Another form of substitution is to try and substitute hateful feelings about yourself with more positive ones. When you are in a crisis it is easy to forget that others love and value you. One suggestion Kharre gives is to prepare an emergency box which is filled with special things associated with positive times in your life or beneficial feelings.[4] When you are feeling low or angry about yourself, it is often very difficult to think of good emotions. This may not always work for you, but the idea of having something which contains objects, letters, or photos of importance to you is a good one. You may find it more helpful to look at it regularly rather than when you are in the midst of a crisis. Again this is most useful when you are beginning to work on communicating how you feel and are receiving feedback from someone who understands you.

4. Recognising and Avoiding Triggers

By recording all the situations, thoughts and feelings that lead up to an episode of self-harm, you can identify what your triggers are. Then you can try and avoid or minimise the impact of factors and situations that you know will disturb you and make it more likely that you will harm yourself. This may involve a very radical change of lifestyle. Common factors that women have identified are:

- alcohol
- drugs (prescribed and illegal)
- friends who self-harm
- contact with specific people, for example a childhood abuser or person who continues to deny your experience of abuse
- being in abusive work situations or other relationships you experience as abusive in some way

Recognising some of the factors that increase your vulnerability to self-harm is extremely important. For example, using alcohol and other drugs facilitates the disconnection between your thinking and feeling self. Used to excess they are both forms of self-harm. Blanking out how you feel is unlikely to resolve the underlying feelings that have led you to self-harm in the first place.

Contact with other women who self-harm may be very beneficial to you but over time it may become less so. You may find you do not continue to make as much progress or that hearing some of the stories from other women makes you feel like self-harming again. Dealing with your own traumatic material will have been stressful enough and you may feel it is time to make a break with the past.

Contact with abusers is extremely toxic. It is very hard to maintain your integrity. Just seeing the person, let alone smelling, hearing, or touching them is likely to bring back many unwanted memories and intense emotional distress. Contact with specific people who continue to deny your experience of abuse can also generate intense feelings that lead to an episode of self-harm.

Tyler was very close to her younger brothers and wanted to see them but her only opportunity to do so was to go to the family home. She felt that her mother refused to believe that she had been sexually abused by her older brother. She felt he was still welcome in her home when she was not; that her parents were proud of him and ashamed of her. After almost every visit she would cut, burn herself or overdose.

> You look at me how you used to when I was a child
> with a mixture of disgust and hatred in your eyes.
> I remember that look so well,
> you seemed to dislike me from the start.
> Now I hate myself,
> direct all my anger at myself, abuse my body
> how he abused me.
> And when I visit your house you have his photograph
>   there
> but not mine,
> you ask me to come to the back door
> so the neighbours will not see me.

As I enter that door my self-hatred builds up inside me,
as I leave I want to die
Did you ever want me to live?

Tyler

If you have to remain in contact with family members
or other people who cause you intense strain, you could
try to find ways of reducing the negative impact they have
on you. For example you could take someone with you.
This would help validate your experience of being with
your family. Alternatively, you could arrange to go and
see members of your family who upset you when you have
also arranged to see someone else who usually has a
positive effect on you. Thereby you both limit your
contact with the family in terms of the time spent with
them and you also have a positive 'antidote' after the visit.

It is not only people from your past that can trigger
you into an episode of self-harm. Events in your present
life can become triggers if they provoke similar feelings in
you. This is most likely to occur within other abusive
relationships or situations but it can also occur if
anything within your current situation causes very
powerful feelings. Learning how to manage these
outbursts in relationships with other people may have
become difficult for you.

The reason today was an argument with my boyfriend.
When I feel emotionally pained, I feel I should be
physically in pain too.

Debbie

Avoidings thing that trigger self-harm need not be for
ever. You may discover that there are times when you are
more vulnerable to the bad effects these factors can have
on you. It is helpful, then, to reassess them from time to
time. Their potency as triggers may change and you may
find that you can, for instance, have a drink without
activating a self-destructive binge, or become involved in

self-help groups without triggering your own traumatic material.

5. Caring for Yourself

Many women who self-harm have become disconnected not only from their feelings of pain and distress but also from normal bodily cues that indicate hunger, cold, fatigue or thirst.

> It reached the stage where I no longer felt physical pain at all.
>
> Sharon

You need to make sure that you eat, sleep and care for your basis physical needs. Many women who self-harm sometimes find it hard to do this. Developmentally, babies rely on a parent, usually mothers, to recognise and meet these essential requirements. If you have a history where these basic needs were not met, or were met unpredictably, you may not have learned how to understand your body cues. You may have to learn to listen to your body. When do you feel hungry and need to eat? What do you want to eat? How often do you need to sleep? How does your body react to changes in temperature? How often are you thirsty? You may have had much greater body awareness as a child before a traumatic event disconnected you from your feelings. Reclaiming that awareness may be really important for you. Take care of yourself when you are ill. If you have people in your life who can care for you, let them. Many women find they don't self-harm when they are ill and this may be because 'physical' illness is more likely to elicit care-taking behaviour from others.

6. Setting Yourself Limits

You may also find it is helpful to put some boundaries around your self-harming behaviour. You probably have some already. This can include making certain places, times or actions out of bounds. You may also start to get rid of some of your self-harming kit or at least not have it always with you.

> I haven't even touched a drink and I got rid of all the dregs in bottles under the bed ages ago. I don't have bottles in my bag! And yesterday I threw away my razor blade, like we talked about. It was a gradual process. I couldn't do it straight away. I used to have it with me at all times. Then I didn't need to have it with me but I needed to know exactly where it was, and now I'm able to throw it away, not have it at all.
>
> Lisa

Equally you may sanction some places – I will only cut in the bathroom, for example. This needs to include some consideration of the context within which you live. For women with children, many would never consider harming themselves in front of them. However, you may have to think how to avoid this as children can accidentally walk in and may have developed a sixth sense about you. They can become very concerned, even overly concerned, and crowd you. This can also be true of partners, parents or friends, and 'crowding' can increase your feelings of tension and push you even closer to episodes of self-harm. But you do need to distinguish between the adult concern of those close to you from that of your children. Children are curious and may ask directly. You may need to think what are you going to say. Your story may need to be different depending on who it is you are speaking to. However, it is important that the story you tell those who care for you does not dismiss or deny the feelings you sometimes have towards yourself, as invalidation of your feelings has had a very significant part in the genesis of your self-harm.

Lapses and Relapse

Whenever any of us begin to make changes in our lives, we can easily lapse back into old familiar patterns of coping. This does not mean we are failures and there is no need to punish ourselves for the lapse – it is completely normal, progress is rarely linear. Don't hide your lapses. You have done nothing wrong. You are not to blame. You have a right to your feelings whatever they may be. Giving up self-harm is a struggle, so use all the help and support you can get. You don't have to keep it all in. You don't have to take it out on yourself.

Sometimes it seems like three steps forward and two back. It feels like the wall is down but the bricks are still there, just in case. I go out for walks but occasionally, when I get very scared I run back and put up a few bricks to hide behind. The difference now is I don't cement them in. I dismantle them and go back out again. I am slowly learning that if I take someone's hand it is less scary and if I do get frightened other people can be more comforting than brick walls.

Cathy

Chapter 7
Family and Friends

Most women who attend A & E departments having self-harmed are in relationships. They have partners, close friends, or children, but very little is written about these people. How they may help. How they may make things worse. How they feel about the self-harm. This is despite the fact that women who self-harm frequently say that worries about their relationships and children, or family conflicts, can be a trigger to an episode of self-harm.[1]

> I'm not close enough to talk to my mum and dad and my two sisters are too young to understand. I wouldn't dream of telling my friends as they see me in a totally different way and we aren't close enough anyway. My boyfriend is the worst though. He really doesn't want to listen and we've had very strong words about it which just makes me more depressed and once or twice I've cut myself over this.
>
> Carly

If you do not self-harm, it can be very difficult to understand why people would or could inflict such injuries on themselves. You may do things that you think are helpful but which in fact seem to make the self-harm worse. You may love the woman deeply but feel repulsed by the injuries she causes and feel hurt and frustrated when she cannot seem to stop herself. You may not understand why she cannot just stop doing it, given how much you care about her and are trying to help her. You may also feel the need for support so that you can cope with the distress and frustration you feel when you see someone you care deeply about hurting themselves so badly.

This chapter looks at some of these issues. Many women who self-harm say that they recognise a great many of the difficulties that those who love them experience. Sometimes they say they fear that the fact they cannot gain control over their self-harm will affect the relationship to such a degree that they will lose the love of the people they need most. In the end the best way forward is so often a supportive partnership. A partnership between a woman who self-harms and those who support her works towards understanding the woman's own specific and unique constellation of factors that increase or reduce the likelihood of her self-harming. It also aims to support her in exploring the origins of her self-harm and developing alternative ways of coping.

> My poor husband felt responsible and must have wondered at times what on earth he had seen in me. I knew my feelings of self-harm were not because of him and if anything he offered me the only stability in my life, so we worked hard at understanding my problem.
>
> Dee

As with the rest of this book the following material is intended to be useful for *both* women who self-harm and those who are in close relationships with them in order to promote greater mutual understanding.

Understanding Why

When you care about someone who self-harms, one way in which you can help both yourself and the person you care about is to understand how her self-harm came about, why and when she does it and what self-harm means for her. Understanding this can also help you understand why certain things that occur within your own relationship which seem quite minor can lead to an episode of self-harm. If you self-harm and have chosen someone to support you as you attempt to give it up, it is important that you feel you can talk openly about these things with the person concerned.

One very influential factor to consider is the relationships within which the self-harm began – whether it arose through an invalidating environment, or through overt experience of emotional, physical or sexual abuse. There may be a multiplicity of explanations as to why someone self-harms. You will need to consider a number of different explanations at different times to see how you can best offer help and support. When you understand why certain things upset the person you are caring for, you will be able to validate their experience and react in a way which they find positive and constructive.

For example, Julie's mother noticed that when Julie was less than five years old, she would often pick scabs off her knees and go to her mother for comforting and cuddles. Julie's mother indulged this behaviour but became more worried when it seemed Julie came more and more often with scratches for her mother to see.

Julie's behaviour continued but initially her mother was unaware that Julie's injuries were self-inflicted. Julie used the blade from her pencil sharpeners at first and later the tops of soft drink cans. The very precise and repeated manner in which the cuts were made, gradually alerted Julie's mother to see that the cuts were self-inflicted. Julie's mother couldn't understand why Julie was doing this. However there was another even more disturbing secret that Julie couldn't tell; Julie's dad was sexually abusing her. When Julie was sixteen years old, and had endured years of sexual abuse, she was finally able to say that this was happening to her, and her mother couldn't believe it. Julie decided to live away from her family and her father remained at home. Julie's self-injuring behaviour became worse and worse involving cutting her arms, legs and stomach with razor blades and glass; punching walls with her fists, starving herself, smoking and drinking excessively.

Julie's experience is very similar to that of many other young women. At first, her mother was sympathetic and responded in a caring and appropriate, perhaps even a slightly indulgent way to her daughter. But over time her mother withdrew this attention and no matter how badly Julie hurt herself she could never recapture the close affectionate moments she had previously enjoyed with her mother.

Julie would feel angry with both herself and her father and direct her angry feelings on to herself. Inflicting the injuries helped to block out thoughts and feelings she had about the sexual abuse. In this way, she was stopping something even more aversive from continuing; her thoughts and feelings about what her father had done to her. This is one of the reasons why Julie continued to self-harm even after the abuse stopped but it puzzled those working with Julie that the episodes of self-harm *increased* in both intensity and severity after she had told her mother. This becomes more understandable when it is recognised that by telling, Julie 'lost' the care and affection of her mother, as her mother found it so difficult to believe what her daughter was saying. Thus as well as losing her source of care and comfort, she also felt betrayed by her mother and had angry and hurt feelings as a result of her mother's reaction.

Later acts of kindness and care intended to comfort Julie reminded her of the 'mother's care' that she had lost. Questions aimed at helping Julie to express how she felt about her sexual abuse may have been unconsciously experienced by Julie as evidence that the person asking did not believe her. She would not have been able to say any of this for fear of further rejection so she 'dealt' with all these feelings by self-harming.

For Julie, like so many women who self-harm, the triggers can be many and varied, and are caused by both internal memories and external events. When you care for someone who self-harms it can be very confusing for both of you as to what exactly the triggers are at any one time. It is helpful if you both can explore, in the most minute detail, all the events, thoughts and feelings leading up to an episode of self-harm, so that you can both understand more clearly what can be done to help.

Helpful Responses

What to Do if Someone You Care for Self-Harms

Sometimes there is no way that a woman can hide the fact that she has self-harmed. More commonly however it is a secret and there are no outward signs that anything has happened.

The trouble with me is that I give the wrong impression to everybody. When I am happy I am very happy but when I am down I am almost at the stage of suicide. People think I haven't a care in the world because that is exactly what I want them to think because I don't want to make anybody worry. My mother worries a lot about me and I know that she would be very upset to know what I have been doing so I carry on pretending that I don't care about anything.

Lisa

Lisa's mother did notice her daughter's cuts on her arms and legs but made sarcastic comments, asking if the cat had scratched her. She also showed no concern about the cuts. When Lisa was 'in care', none of the staff commented on them either. So despite the cuts being plainly visible, no one felt able to mention them.

Sometimes people feel that if they make comments they will cause embarrassment. However, if you do notice, and if you are emotionally close to the person involved it is important for you to comment and convey your concern. If you know that someone has a history of self-harming behaviour, and you also know it has been a particularly stressful time for the individual, it is helpful to ask if she wants to talk, or if she has been hurting herself. It can be a relief for someone who self-harms to have others ask, rather than having to make the effort to bring up the subject themselves or show their injuries to someone. It can be so healing when someone bears witness to the emotional pain endured and offers the appropriate response that should have been forthcoming long ago.

I tried to keep my problems to myself but a friend noticed my wrist when my sleeve fell down at school. She was very supportive and made me promise not to do it again and gradually I got over the depression.

Rebecca

The woman who self-harms needs care and attention if she is going to recover.[2] Being told 'There, now it's over' is not as helpful as 'Let me help make it better' which at least recognises the hurt behind the injury. If you self-harm and you feel that those closest to you do not recognise the intensity of your anguish, it is advisable to look for other sources of support, such as self-help groups.

> Personally I found that love was my cure. I wanted someone to love...I am now very happily married to a loving, gentle and understanding man who I met whilst in hospital. We have helped each other a great deal and I feel I am very lucky to have found love at last. Love is my cure.
>
> Nicki

Loving and caring for a woman who self-harms is a very important factor in her recovery, but it is only in very rare cases that this alone is enough to stop her from hurting herself. Therefore you should not feel that, when a woman continues to self-harm, she is rejecting your love and attention. Most women need to look specifically at the triggers to their self-harm, what it means to them and to develop other ways of expressing their feelings.

Getting the Message: What is Being Said That Cannot Be Spoken?

Dusty Miller, who wrote *Women who Hurt Themselves*, sees self-harming behaviour as a means of representing symbolically what has been done to you.[3] Other people who have thought and written about self-harm have reached similar conclusions.[4] These writers say that person who self-harms needs to be held, cuddled and comforted. However, the person themselves may or may not initially be able to cope with that physical contact as it may trigger feelings of distress.

If you can both begin to see the injuries as a message and explore what that message means then you can begin to discover other more appropriate ways of expressing it and making others hear it.

People just aren't aware of the pain involved in this and should understand it isn't just a means of getting attention as people are inclined to think, but it shows a lot of pain, distress, anger and tension within a person who does it. They should understand that cutting yourself shows a person who is hurting badly inside and can't express it.

Melanie

One useful strategy is for the carer to ask how did the woman feel just before she hurt herself? Just after? Now? Can she put her feelings into words? Or pictures? Can she share in any way what was going through her mind when she hurt herself? What might have been bothering her?

On other occasions a more direct approach is helpful. What are you trying to get rid of? Cut out? Burn off? (Depending on the type of injury.) If you cannot verbalise these thoughts and feelings at the time, your carer may be able to encourage you to write down your thoughts so that you can discuss them together at a later date.

I always try to make time to talk to Ann about what has distressed her especially if I know she has cut up. A lot of the time though she doesn't seem to know – it is as if she becomes so disconnected from herself that she can't remember what it was exactly. I try to help by sharing my thoughts and observations about what might have been the triggers but I worry even in doing that that I will somehow trigger another episode of self-harm. That's my worry though it seems to help her make sense of what is going on and it is comforting to her to know that at least I can see what's happening to her.

Carer

Sometimes a woman who self-harms does not know exactly why she does it, and so she cannot even explain it to herself let alone the people who care about her. For example Steph had been in therapy for a long time before she was able to make the connection between witnessing her father's death by stabbing, and being forbidden to talk about his death, with her self-harm. She says that she now thinks it is extremely obvious and has trouble understanding why she did not make the connection before. Her difficulty in explaining her behaviour also had an impact on her husband:

> I never really understood Steph's need not only to cut herself but to smear the blood all over her body. The cuts were bad enough but I found her need to smear the blood all over her so repulsive. It was hard to sleep in the same bed as her knowing she had done that. I tried to hide my repulsion but knew she must sense it. I love her so much but just could not understand this part of her. It also made me feel angry with myself. It was only after Steph had been in therapy for a year or so and began to be able to talk about seeing her father stabbed to death and how her body became covered in his blood that it began to make sense to me. That somehow stopped the repulsion straight away. I understood.
>
> Tony – Steph's Husband

It is often better to separate the caring for the injury from talking about what led up to it, otherwise you could be setting up a connection between talking about feelings and being cared for after an injury that might be unhelpful or replicate a past pattern. Part of helping someone not to self-harm is to encourage them to talk about their feelings *before* they self-harm. You may want to schedule regular talking times, that are not contingent on an episode of self-harm.

Assessing Damage

When a woman self-harms, the most urgent thing to do is to assess the damage and decide what treatment the injuries need. It is important that first aid equipment is available but you should also determine whether or not professional help is needed. This assessment is very dependent on the individual who self-harms, and her judgement as to the severity of her injuries.

If you are caring for a young person who cannot judge the severity of the wound, you may need to see the injury to make an assessment of what should be done next. You should be prepared to deal with any feelings of disgust and fear which might arise. You need to make it clear that you are not disgusted by the person, but are over-whelmed by the injury and the pain it must be causing. If you are squeamish this can be especially difficult.

> I can remember being asked by a friend to see her photographic essay on self-harming entitled 'Strong in the Weak Places' (Ethel Findlay). I admit to intense feelings of squeamishness. However, her photos were of the scars, all in various stages of healing and I was curious, intrigued and inspired by the images she had created with the photographs. When I look at injuries now, I try to think what they are saying or feeling for the woman. Sometimes I ask her about specific scars as I often find they each have a story to tell – often a story that has not been told before.
>
> Carer

Setting Limits

The importance of having people in your life who you feel close to, and in whom you can confide, is seen as vital in maintaining good mental health and particularly in warding off depression.[5] Not surprisingly, women who self-harm say that being able to talk to someone is one of the ways they can resist an episode of self-harm. However, even those who do have close confiding relationships say they found it difficult to contact people who said that they would support them, as they found that many of their crises happened late at night. If you are trying to support someone who self-harms, you need to be clear how available you can be to them. Are you prepared to be woken in the middle of the night, when the thoughts and feelings are often at their worse, and the possibility of harming oneself feels irresistible? Could there be other people also available for support, so that the responsibility for being contactable at night is shared?

> I had a brilliant CPN who saved the day on more than one occasion by listening to me ranting on down the end of a telephone until the moment of crisis had passed. I always found it difficult to tell my partner how bad I felt. I think it was because I didn't want to load any more problems on to his broad shoulders.
>
> Dee

While not condoning self-harm, in the short term it may be unavoidable, and it is important that you help manage it as safely as possible, until it stops. Therefore you might want to discuss with the person who self-harms the possibility of setting some parameters around self-harming behaviour that you feel you can manage.

Unhelpful Responses

Many women who self-harm experience very angry and rejecting responses from friends and family when their self-harm is discovered. They become very astute at hiding the evidence, as they have been met with, or expect to be met with, rejection and a lack of understanding.

> Recently when I'd cut myself, my friend who'd previously been really helpful didn't know what to do and she said 'You've got lots of friends, you shouldn't do something stupid like that.'
>
> Rebecca

Over time it can become easier to pretend it isn't happening at all or any more.

I've lost friends as a result and the ones who are still there, avoid the subject like the plague and I'm glad they do now.

Christine

Even people who were previously very supportive can become frustrated and exasperated by the continuing self-harm and withdraw support or become controlling.

My boyfriend was just so upset and he said that if I did it again, he'd finish with me. Sometimes I wear long-sleeved pyjamas but his hands still feel the cuts. Anyway this time he made me go to the doctor.

Carly

It may seem impossible to strike the balance between clearly stating you do not want someone to self-harm and you want to help them stop, yet at the same time conveying the message that you totally accept the woman as she is and recognise that there may be times when she will find it impossible not to self-harm. It is important to accept that someone who self-harms is a person who manages their feelings in the best way they can. This may, from time to time, result in self-harm until they can find other ways of managing or controlling their feelings. If you self-harm, you should remember that people supporting you will make mistakes, and you should try and tell them if they upset you, or if you feel judged or misunderstood. As a carer, if you respond to self-harm by being very controlling, you can make the behaviour worse. When some women are stopped from self-harming they have found that the next episode of self-harm is even more serious.

I've observed that the longer I suppress the urge, the worse the injuries at the next session are.

Christine

Family, friends and partners of those who self-harm can become very involved in helping them stop. However, often the major strategy is to remove the instrument of the self-harm, such as blades or poisons. This is counterproductive and tends to lead to an escalation in the self-harm.

> She took all my blades but I couldn't stop. Not having them made it worse but I got more. She searched my room everyday, she told me if I did it again I would have to leave. All that did was make me more and more secretive and determined to cut. I cut more often, in more and more secret places on my body. I felt more obsessed with cutting at that time than I ever have.
>
> Steph
> (Describing her mother's attempts to control her self-harm)

It is far better to try to deal with the triggers and feelings that provoke the episode in the first place. By trying to control the environment and make it safe, you are inadvertently depriving the woman of developing her own self-control.

> I've cut up and told my mum. She's bandaged me up and then we've sat down and talked. They never condemned me and though it has been terrible for them just to sit back and let me do it, they realise I need to work through this in my own time. Because they don't judge me, they've helped me through it.
>
> Holly[6]

When you care deeply about someone, it is difficult to contain feelings of disappointment and even frustration and anger when that person cuts, burns, ingests poisons or self-harms in other ways, rather than coming to talk to you about how they feel. You can feel rejected, as if the care, time and affection you give her are not good enough to stop her hurting herself. When this happens you might withdraw, even unconsciously, and this in turn makes the woman you care about feel rejected. Rejection, whether perceived or real by the person you feel closest to is terribly painful and can be a trigger to self-harm. If feelings of rejection continue, hopelessness can set in and this is a very real danger. It is also true that, if you self-harm, you need to remember that the person supporting you needs to feel accepted too. It is so important that if you are close to someone who self-harms, you have a chance to express all the frustrations and tensions the situation brings so that these feelings are not stored up, or 'leaked out' through hostile and critical comments. If someone who self-harms lives in an environment where there are high levels of hostile comments, they are much less likely to get better.

Louise Pembroke in her book, *Self-harm: Perspectives from Personal Experience*, gives clear advice on what is helpful and unhelpful if you are in a close relationship with someone who self-harms. She offers the following suggestions to relatives and friends:

1. Don't reject
2. Don't give ultimatums
3. Offer moral support and/or possible advocacy when dealing with medical personnel
4. Don't assume that when someone isn't self-harming they don't need your support.
5. Don't give up, especially when the medical services have.

We would like to add another: Make sure you have some support for yourself. Somewhere you can put your feelings.

Support for Caregivers

Little is written about the pain and anguish you can experience when you love someone who self-harms. It can seem that no matter how hard you try, you always get it wrong. If you take blades away, you are being controlling. If you leave them, you are being unfeeling. If you say nothing, you are insensitive. If you comment you are intrusive. This is a no-win situation.

My mum came into the room offering advice but I just turned her down. As soon as she left the room, I felt an overwhelming anger, at who or what I don't know but I cut up really badly.

Carly

Ann phoned one evening. I could tell immediately that she was in a state. She had hurt herself. She wanted me to come over but she would not have asked. She was scared because her injury was still bleeding. When I arrived she was in a very agitated state. I looked at her cut which needed stitches. She was adamant she would not go to A & E. She continued to pace and I knew she would not calm down. It was like she was in another world. Nothing I said seemed to reach her. I dealt with the first aid, tending to her wound. When I left her she was still in a state but I felt there was nothing more I could do. I would just have to wait and hope her anxiety would pass. She was hospitalised a few days later.

Carer

You can also worry that you are making things worse, or say something in anger that you regret. Often the overwhelming feeling you might have is to leave the relationship, as managing the complexities is just too difficult.

In the middle of a row, he suggested I should try a chemical I hadn't thought of before. I stormed off and painted some onto my arm and left it there to see what it would do.

Dee

As a carer you can begin to think you are the problem. Or you can experience a very blaming and dismissive attitude from professionals who are 'treating' the woman; as if you are both the cause of the self-harming behaviour, and are inadequate for not stopping it. These feelings can be conveyed to you both verbally and non verbally. This is a typical response in A & E departments, or when the woman is admitted to a psychiatric ward.

> It was the third night of the week that I'd had to take Tyler to hospital. The first two times we had been up no one said anything negative to me but they made their feelings obvious. On the third night the staff nurse clearly lost her temper. She shouted at me that they had better things to do and if I couldn't look after her properly she'd be better off on her own or I should ask social services to place her with someone who could look after her.
>
> Carer

There is an enormous need for support groups, not only for women who self-harm but also for those who care for them. Such a group should provide a safe place for supporters to share their feelings of helplessness, despair and anger. There are, however, very few groups available. You may be able to use the telephone help-lines set up for people who self-harm, but to our knowledge there are none that have been set up specifically for supporters. One source of support and information that is available to those who have access to a computer and to the Internet, is a message board specifically for people who care for and support someone who self-harms.[7] It is full of messages and requests for help.

Another option is to try and find someone in a similar position and develop a co-support system whereby you meet on a regular basis for a set period of time. Each person uses half that time to give support and the other half to get support. Some people are fortunate enough to have someone they can turn to for support on a regular basis. Counselling should be more available than it is, as it is a very effective and beneficial use of resources. However, services are already stretched and unfortunately professional help is rarely available. Nevertheless, it is worthwhile putting your case for some professional support to your GP who might be able to arrange it for you. Another possibility is to ask your local Relate or the Samaritans if they could provide regular support.

> Steph was seeing a therapist based at the hospital. Working with Steph she realised how difficult what Steph was doing was for me to deal with. I wanted to help her so much but I just got angry. I couldn't do right for doing wrong. The therapist arranged for me to see the CPN in the team once a month. It made all the difference. I could tell her how I felt and she would help me understand what was happening with Steph as well. I really don't think we'd have made it without her.
>
> Tony – Steph's husband

Never underestimate the support, care, attention and affection that a woman who self-harms will need to help her recover. Equally, never underestimate the necessity for support for yourself. In order for you to provide the unconditional positive regard, care and compassion that is required to heal self-harming behaviour, you must have a place to replenish your own life-giving energy.

Afterword

Whether you are a person who self-harms or a person who cares for someone who does, self-harm can be overwhelming. You can find yourself challenged by its intensity. It is almost as if self-harm has a life of its own, throwing you and those around you into a maelstrom of conflicting, confusing advice and a myriad of experiences where it is difficult to seperate out the good from the bad. Sometimes it may seem you cannot control self-harm and nothing will ever change. There are no easy answers nor instant treatments. However, women can and do stop self-harming. It is often a long journey; more of a marathon than a sprint.

I self-harmed for more than twenty years and I felt like I'd been trying to stop myself doing it for most of that time. Back and forwards to casualty, seeing psychiatrists, making pacts with myself to stop and then hating myself more for failing, seeing a couple of counsellors, one who seemed terrified of me and one who seemed to want to punish me if I harmed myself so I stopped telling her. But I've stopped doing it now, part of me can't believe that I have, yet it's now almost three years since I last self-harmed. I was in therapy for just over four years, sometimes I felt like giving up especially when about a year after I started therapy my self-harm seemed to get worse not better. It's like, I feel in control, I feel that I'm really living life now.

Lucy

In looking back and reflecting on what we have written, we can see how much greater our own understanding of self-harm has become over the years. Almost all of what we know we have learnt from those women who have had the courage to share their memories, their thoughts, and their feelings with us. Some of those women no longer need to self-harm, others now self-harm much less, others are still in the process of working through their problems.

You are the only one who has expert knowledge of yourself. What we have tried to provide in this book is a framework within which you can place your own experiences, and some suggestions as to possible routes to recovery.

Just as there is no one route to recovery, there is no one definitive reason why a woman self-harms. The different meanings for your injuries are often not appreciated. The explanations we have given are multifaceted and complex. A simple answer will not explain a complex phenomena.

I wanted it to be simple, like I was ill, depressed, or even mad, I wanted there to be something diagnosable wrong with me so that I could just be given some drug and I would stop doing this to myself.

Debbie

Like all complex situations, self-harm cannot be resolved overnight. You will have setbacks and relapses but that certainly does not mean you have failed – it is all

part of the gradual process of recovery. The important
thing is not to blame yourself. Women tend to feel that,
whenever there is a problem, we are somehow at fault;
we believe it is because there is something wrong with us.
The more that we try to conquer that problem and fail,
the more guilty we feel. It is likely that when trying to
find alternative ways of coping with your pain, you *will*
lapse back into self-harm on occasion, and then feel
angry with yourself. Sometimes this belief is reinforced
by those who are supposed to care for you,
professionally and personally. Their own feelings of
helplessness, powerlessness, fear, confusion, and lack of
understanding about the injuries can become confused
with yours. This is a common response, but is ultimately
unhelpful. Being blamed, or rejected or punished by
those around you each time you have a setback can feel
like a continuation of earlier experiences and reactions.

Do my scars embarrass you so much?
You make me feel like you do not want me near you.
The look on your face, your posture, the movement of
your body speak only of disgust.
I feel so alienated from you.
Like I was so alienated from my family,
particularly my mother.
She never heard my fear, my pain, my shame
but was disgusted by me too.
I learnt to stay silent, and now
it is so much easier to let blood flow than words.

Tyler

The roots of self-injury come well before the first cut.
The more we learn about self-harm, the more we realise
the part played by the attitudes, beliefs and behaviours of
the society in which we live. In a society which continues
to minimise care and nurturing, placing competition and
survival of the fittest above compassion and social

responsibility, it is easy to see why some women feel they can only express their pain and distress through injuring themselves. As our society is so dominated by 'lookism', perhaps showing our pain on the outside is a form of 'cosmetic surgery' where our inner person can finally be seen and recognised. It may even be an act of rebellion.

> I never tried to hide my scars. I wanted them to show yet I could see the disgust in people's eyes when they saw my wounds and I would then withdraw again behind my wall as if they sent me there. I knew understanding why I did this was going to be very important if I was going to stop.
>
> Cathy

Showing pain in a society that does not want to hear of too much suffering is a difficult thing to do. Seeing another person's suffering is uncomfortable and often leads to ideas of contagion, as if in looking, seeing and responding we might in some way increase the risk of self-harm for ourselves. People turn away from the unpleasant nature of self-harm, but the woman herself experiences this as a withdrawal of support, care and compassion. This sort of reaction only increases the need to self-harm and interferes with the process of recovery. People need to be educated to respond differently and supported so that they can understand their reactions.

All of us have a role to play in one woman's recovery. Pain, suffering and violence are everywhere. We are exposed to more of it through the medium of television, photojournalism, and now the Internet. If, as a society, we do not learn to develop, and elaborate our compassionate, protecting repertoire, it is almost inevitable that self-harm will continue to disturb potential helpers, and destroy the lives of many more women.

Through therapy many women come to understand that one of the motivations to self-harm may be anger with a world that they feel does not understand them; does not believe they have been abused or hurt by others who should have cared: *'I wanted someone to recognise I had been hurt, that it wasn't my fault, and care about me.'* Recognition of the hurt in and of itself is helpful. Continued denial of it leads to further despair.

Unfortunately, many people in our society do believe that individuals are in some way responsible for the abuse they experience, that they must have in some way contributed to it, or deserved it. It seems more comforting to believe this than to put the issue of blame and responsibility for abuse with those who perpetrate it. By subscribing to victim-blaming beliefs, so often voiced by perpetrators of such crimes, people can delude themselves with the idea that they, and their children, can avoid being abused by not being like those who have been; victims are 'not like us'. If victims self-harm, the self-harm can be interpreted as a form of punishment and further evidence of their complicity in the original abusive acts. This attitude allows society as a whole to effectively relieve itself of any responsibility in alleviating the causes of self-harm.

After almost three years of not harming myself I found myself standing there again covered in blood. I couldn't believe that I'd done it. It happened after my youngest sister Tilly had come to tell me that our parents had also sexually abused her. I had told what they were doing to me, but I wasn't believed and Tilly was left there with them. I became obsessed with the idea that if only they had not seen *me* as the problem, and believed me about my abuse, the same thing would not have happened to Tilly, she would have been safe. Over the next weeks I found myself back in my old pattern. I was so angry. I eventually phoned the woman who had been my therapist and she agreed to see me again. After a few sessions I stopped self-harming. Even though that was a year ago, I feel more vulnerable than I did, less sure that self-harm will not intrude into my life again.

Cathy

Beginning to self-harm after a period of not doing so does not mean that you cannot go back again to using less destructive ways of coping, either alone or with someone's help. It is important not to give up. Try and make sense of what triggered the new episode. The more you understand about yourself, the more choices you will be able to make in your life and the more you can express yourself in other ways.

Steph, who at the age of four had witnessed the stabbing of her father, described her own personal journey towards recovery and self-awareness:

My first real memory of deliberate self-harm is when I was about eleven. I was sitting in my room just thinking about my dad and how he died. It would often happen. I would be just doing everyday normal things and then I'd get these images of his body covered in blood in my mind. After that I would scratch myself and the scrates became cuts and the cuts became deeper.

My mother tried to stop me but I kept finding new ways and places to cut myself. She went to the GP and told him I needed help but I refused to go and see him or anyone else. The older I got the worse it seemed to get.

When I met Tony, I thought that falling in love would end the need to do it and it sort of did for a while. He made me feel so good. I told him about the cutting, I couldn't hide the scars. I felt that I'd stopped doing it but I knew I was fooling myself really. After we got married it started again. I suddenly became terrified of losing Tony. I'd get tense and worked up. I ended up cutting, not badly at first but then it got worse and the trips to Casualty began again.

Tony was supportive at first and then we started having terrible rows about it. The more we rowed the more rejected I felt, the more I did it which just caused more rows. I knew I had to accept help this time. I went into hospital which was a waste of time. Then I was sent to a day hospital. It didn't seem to help at all but it was there that I began to see a therapist. At first I didn't really think that would help but she was so patient. I hadn't even connected the cutting to my father's death; I did not have any words for how I felt – just images and terrible feelings. The night I told her about my dad's murder I ended up in hospital again I cut myself so badly.

I had to learn what I was feeling and why. That was really hard and I was in therapy for almost three years. I was so scared it would never end. I felt as if it controlled me. Tony and I were struggling, so my therapist arranged for him to see someone and that seemed to help so much. He began to try and help me more; to talk things through with me.

My life has changed so much. It is now years since I last self-harmed. I have a baby son who is now eight months. I still have times when I feel tense and stressed but I've found other ways of dealing with those feelings. In the short term I distract myself, take the baby for a walk, exercise, clean and then, when I can, I talk about my feelings. I can cry now, really, really cry, and get comfort from Tony and my friends. I feel free now, really free, and in control.

Steph

It is our hope that in reading the words and experiences of others there may be the flash of recognition, a connection that tells you that you are not alone, and that others have also sought solace through acts of self-harm – crazy as that may seem. Other women have also turned their feelings inward, having absorbed messages of misogyny that tacitly support women harming themselves.

The debate about self-harm needs to be widened and those who do not self-harm have got to start asking why so many people do and what is going to be done about it. This requires courage and resilience – attributes often in short supply. If you are struggling in terms of your day to day existence, you cannot afford to squander these resources. Yet the push for better services so often comes from the women who use them. In the same way that female survivors put sexual abuse on the mental health map, women who self-harm are creating a growing awareness of their own needs. In doing so there will be both good and bad developments, as the mental health professionals co-opt some of our best efforts and avoid some of our most important demands such as 24-hour phone lines, and an acknowledgement of the wider political and social implications of self-harm. Trying to find a balance between claiming your own expertise and being able to use that of others will be a constant challenge, and perhaps one initially viewed with mutual suspicion on both sides. Yet self-harm is too complex to ignore possible avenues of support.

This book aims to even up the playing field – to enable you to identify your own patterns of behaviour, to understand how you may be viewed within psychiatric services and to increase your awareness about what support may be available to you. We have also tried to elaborate on theories of self-harm that emphasise the biological processes involved. By harming your physical self in response to psychological distress, your body naturally and instinctively responds to such assaults. In part we need to learn to respond instinctively to psychological hurt in much the same way, healing and defending ourselves from long-term psychological harm.

This will mean learning not to be so 'nice' as in doing so we often put other people's feelings before our own, and as a consequence hurt ourselves. We are then 'rewarded' for such female altruism without the real cost of the altruism being recognised.

This book is also meant to encourage you to identify others who can help you break the habit of self-harm – whether it is a professional who works within mental health, your partner, parent or friend. For those of you who care for or support someone who self-harms, we hope it provides an opportunity to either consolidate what you have learned already or to begin to understand more of the issues involved in self-harming. You may be the only person who sees the woman you support as a whole being, someone capable of a great range of expression of feeling, including compassion, humour and warmth – feelings that may not be in evidence to those who care for her when she is feeling her worst or most vulnerable.

We wish we could write of magic cures and happy endings but our experience tells us it will be a struggle to break self-harming habits. Nevertheless, it is a struggle worth having. The importance of knowing at least one person who unconditionally keeps on fighting for you, believes in you and wants the best for you is the beginning of self-love. It is an experience we should all have as a right. For those who have learned to live without it, it is the greatest gift anyone can give.

Notes

Chapter 1: What is Self-Harm and Who Does It?

1   For a much greater elaboration of many of the issues see the excellent book *The Language of Injury: Comprehending Self-Mutilation* by G. Babiker and L. Arnold, BPS Books, Leicester, 1997.

2   A.R. Favazza and K. Conterio, 'Female Habitual Self-Mutilators', *Acta Psychiatrica Scandinavica* 79 (1989), pp.283–9.

3   S. Herpertz, 'Self-Injurious Behaviour', *Acta Psychiatrica Scandinavica* 91 (1981) pp.57–68.

4   B. Burstow, *'Self Mutilation' in Radical Feminist Therapy*, Sage, California, 1992, p.188.

5   G. M. de Moore and A. R. Robertson, 'Suicide in the 18 years after Deliberate Self-Harm', *British Journal of Psychiatry* 169 (1996), pp.489–94.

6   G. Babiker and L. Arnold, op cit.

7   D. Tantum and J. Whittaker, 'Personality Disorder and Self-wounding', *British Journal of Psychiatry* 161 (1992), pp.451–64.

8   K. Hawton and J. Catalan, *Attempted Suicide*, Oxford University Press, 1987.

9   Concepts such as 'new man' and 'new lad' reflect this changing ethos.

10   G. Babiker and L. Arnold, op cit.

11   See for example, 'Coffee Coloured Children', a video which describes the experience of two young black children living with their white mother.

12   e.g. E.M. Pattison and J. Kahan, 'The Deliberate Self-Harm Syndrome', *American Journal of Psychiatry* 140 (1983), pp.867–72.

13   K. Hawton, J. Fagg and S. Simkin, 'Deliberate Self-Poisoning and Self-Injury in Children and Adolescents Under 16 Years of Age in Oxford 1976–1993', *British Journal of Psychiatry* 169 (1996), pp.202–208.

14   B. A. van der Kolk, 'Complexity of Adaptation to Trauma', in *Traumatic Stress: The Effects of Overwhelming Experience on Mind, Body and Society*, B.A. van der Kolk, A.C. McFarlane and L. Weisaeth, eds, Guildford Press, New York, 1996.

15   B. Burstow, op cit.

16   C.A. Simpson and G. L. Porter, 'Self Mutilation in Children and Adolescents', *Bulletin of the Menninger Clinic* 45 (1981), pp.428–38.

17   B.A. van der Kolk, C. Perry and J. Herman, 'Childhood Origins of Self-Destructive Behavior', *American Journal of Psychiatry* 148 (1991), pp.1665–71.

18   B.A. van der Kolk, A.C. McFarlane and L. Weisaeth, op cit.

Chapter 2: Explanations of Self-Harm

1   This is a paraphrasing of the DSM III *Diagnostic and Statistical Manual of Mental Disorders*, 3rd Edition Revised, American Psychiatric Association, Washington DC, 1987, p.305.

2   J. Herman, *Trauma and Recovery*, HarperCollins, London, 1992, p.123.

3   M. H. Stone, 'A Psychodynamic Approach', *Journal of Personality Disorders* 1 (1987), pp.347–9.
4   J. Herman, op cit.
5   M. Linehan, *Cognitive Behavioural Treatment of Borderline Personality Disorder*, Guilford Press, New York, 1993.
6   See in particular B.A. van der Kolk, A.C. McFarlane and L. Weisaeth, eds, op cit.
7   B. Burstow, op cit, p.195.
8   J. Kroll, *PTSD/Borderlines in Therapy*, W.W. Norton, London, 1993.
9   J. Herman, op cit.
10 E. Peled, P. Jaffee, J. Edleson, eds, *Ending the Cycle of Violence*, Sage, London, 1995.
11 G. Babiker and L. Arnold, op cit.
12 D. Miller, *Women who Hurt Themselves: A Book of Hope and Understanding*, Basic Books, New York, 1994.

Chapter 3: Getting Access to Services

1   See the resources section for addresses where you can check qualifications and membership.
2   There is currently much debate over the terminology used to describe those who make use of the National Health Service. We have chosen to use 'client' as this emphasises the fact that the health authority is providing a service and avoids the connotations of illness and disease associated with the term 'patient'.
3   L. Pembroke 'Surviving Psychiatry', *Nursing Times* 87, No. 49 (1991), pp.30–2.
4   G. Babiker and L. Arnold, op cit.
5   Ibid.
6   D. Dawson, 'Treatment of the Borderline Patient, Relationship Management', *Canadian Journal of Psychiatry* 33 (1988), pp.370–74.
7   MIND Information Line can provide you with details of local MIND Associations.

8   M. Moffaert 'Self-Mutilation: Diagnosis and Practical Treatment', *International Journal of Psychiatry in Medicine* 20, No. 4 (1990), pp.373–82.

Chapter 4: Conventional Treatments

1   L. Pembroke, ed, *Self-Harm: Perspectives from Personal Experience*, Survivors Speak Out, London, 1994, p.35.
2   Ibid (from the dedication).
3   Gina Hills, *Nursing Times* 83, No. 18, (6 May 1990).
4   Mental Health Foundation, 'Knowing Our Own Minds: A survey of how people in emotional distress take control of their lives', 1997. The address of the Mental Health Foundation is in the Resources Section.
5   Ibid.
6   There are some specific treatments that have been identified as helpful in processing trauma although these are still relatively new in the UK. They include EMDR (Eye Movement Desensitisation and Reprocessing), TFT (Thought Field Therapy) and V/KD (visual/kinaesthetic dissociation which is akin to Eriksonian hypnosis). These may be available at clinics that specialise in trauma work.
7   G. Babiker and L. Arnold, op cit.
8   Ibid, p.127.
9   Ibid, p.129.
10   Ibid, pp.133–4.
11   M. Linehan, op cit.
12   M. Webster 'Emotional Abuse in Therapy', *A.N.Z. Journal of Family Therapy* 12, No. 3 (1991), pp.137–45.
13   POPAN Prevention of Professional Abuse Network exists specifically to provide information and support for people who have been abused by professionals. Their address is in the Resources Section.
14   C.B. Truax and R. Carkhuff, *Towards Effective Counselling and Psychotherapy*, Aldine, Chicago 1967.

15 S. Fernando, ed, *Mental Health in a Multi Ethnic Society*, Routledge, London, 1995.

Chapter 5: Self-Help

1 C. Pelikan, Speaker, First National Conference, September 1989.
2 This was also Dee's experience.
3 These cards are available from Survivors Speak Out, 34 Osnaburgh Street, London NW1 3ND.

Chapter 6: Disrupting Self-Harm Patterns

1 See for example B. Azar, 'The body can become addicted to self injury', 1995, reported in the APA Monitor on the Internet (www.apa.org/monitor/dec95/selfhurt.html) or B.A. van der Kolk, 'The Body Keeps the Score: Memory and the Evolving Psychobiology of Post-Traumatic Stress', *Harvard Review of Psychiatry* 1, No. 5 (1995), pp.253–65.
2 M. Linehan, op cit.
3 D. Miller, op cit.
4 Kharre, op. cit.

Chapter 7: Family and Friends

1 J. Brooking and E. Minghella, 'Parasuicide', *Nursing Times* 83, No. 21, (27 May 1987).
2 The Bristol Crisis Centre address is in the Resources Section.
3 D. Miller, op cit.
4 H. Graff and R. Mallin, 'The Syndrome of the Wristcutter' quoted in A.K. Gardiner and A.J. Gardiner, *British Journal of Psychiatry* 127 (1967), pp.127–32.
5 G.W. Brown and T. Harris, *Social Origins of Depression*, London, Tavistock, 1978; G.W. Brown, B. Andrews, T. Harris, J. Adler and L. Bridge 'Social Support, Self Esteem and Depression', *Psychological Medicine* 16 (1986), pp.813–31.

6   Quoted in an article by Maggie Ross entitled 'Shocking Habit'.
7   The message board at the website http://crystal. palace.net/~llama/psych/injury.html

Appendix I
Drugs Commonly Prescribed to Women Who Self-Harm

Almost all women who have approached medical professionals have, at some time, been prescribed at least one form of drug therapy. Although some of these drugs are more helpful than others, there is no evidence that any medication currently available can consistently control self-harming behaviour.

1. Anti-depressants

Traditionally self-harm has been seen as an indication of a woman's low mood and poor self-esteem and so women who self-harm have been prescribed anti-depressant medication.

Tricyclic anti-depressants (e.g. imipramine, amitriptyline, doxepine)
Some GPs and psychiatrists may offer this form of medication although there is no evidence that it reduces self-harming behaviours.
Common Side Effects – dry mouth, blurred vision, dizziness, lowered blood pressure, appetite changes, insomnia

Monoaime oxidase inhibitors (e.g. iproniazid, phenelzine)
These are an older form of anti-depressant which for
some years have been far less popular than the tricyclic
anti-depressants. This is mainly due to the fact that they
have severe and dangerous side effects when taken with
several common foods such as Marmite, hard cheeses,
broad beans and bananas as well as beer and some wines.
However, more recently the use of these drugs with
appropriate dietary restrictions has again become
popular as they have been shown to be useful in treating
a range of behaviour including self-harm.
*Common Side Effects – dry mouth, nausea, dizziness,
restlessness, fatigue*

**Serotonin uptake inhibitors (e.g. fluoxetine (Prozac),
clomipramine)**
The research indicates that self-harming behaviour is
associated with a decrease in the function of a brain
chemical called serotonin. Therefore drugs that increase
this brain chemical logically should reduce the need to
self-harm. Several studies have shown that use of these
drugs in high doses did significantly reduce self-harm.
*Common Side Effects – nausea, headache, insomnia,
sexual dysfunction*

2. Tranquillisers

Another name for tranquillisers is anxiolytics. These drugs
are designed to reduce anxiety and are therefore sometimes
prescribed to women who self-harm as it is believed that if
they are less anxious and thus are less emotionally aroused,
theoretically they will self-harm less.

Minor Tranquillisers

**Benzodiazepines (e.g. diazepam (Valium), lorazepam,
(Activan))**
Although these drugs reduce anxiety and thus emotional

tension there is little evidence that they reduce self-harming behaviour. In fact in some cases, self-harming behaviour was seen to increase.

Common Side Effects – dizziness headache, nausea, psychological dependency, attention and memory impairments, drowsiness

Serotonin related tranquillisers (e.g. buspirone)

Although there has been no reported trials of this tranquilliser used with women who self-harm, it is possible that it may be more useful than other minor tranquillisers as it increases the levels of the brain chemical serotonin. It also has fewer side effects and is safer in overdoses than the benzodiazepines.

Common Side Effects – rare but can be dizziness, headaches and nausea

Major Tranquillisers

(e.g. thoridazine (Meleril), chlorpromazine (Largactyl))

The major tranquillisers are often given in desperation when minor tranquillisers have proved to be ineffective. Major tranquillisers can in fact reduce self-harming behaviour in some people but the side effects have a profoundly detrimental effect on the person's quality of life.

Common Side Effects – dry mouth, sedation, apathy, sensitivity to light, hypotension, mental depression

3. Sedatives

Benzodiazepines (e.g. termazepan); other sedatives (e.g. chloral hydrate)

Some women have been prescribed sedatives in the hope these would calm their tension and help them relax or sleep. Paradoxically in some cases the use of these drugs

has been found to *increase* self-harming behaviour. This is thought to be because these drugs reduce inhibition.
Common Side Effects *– hangover type symptoms, over-sedation, abdominal pain*

4. Other medications that have been shown to be effective in some cases

The two drugs that have mostly consistently been found to be effective in reducing self-harming behaviour are lithium carbonate and carbamazine. Both these drugs are traditionally given to people who suffer from manic-depression. How these drugs affect the brain is not fully understood but both have been shown to be effective at reducing self-harming behaviour in some cases.
Common Side Effects *– loss of ability to co-ordinate muscles, urinary frequency, slurred speech*

5. Opiate Receptor Blockers

Self-harming behaviour has been shown to bring about a feeling of calm. Research has shown that this sense of calm is due to the release of endogenous opioids; opiate-like chemicals that occur naturally in the brain. Just as people can become addicted to other opioids such as heroine, opium and morphine, so they can become addicted to the release of their endogenous opioids. If addicted, the person can also suffer from a feeling of 'withdrawal' which leads them to engage in behaviour that in the past has led to the release of these chemicals.

Judith Herman and her colleagues carried out some trials in which people who self-harmed were given a drug (naltrexone) that reduced the need in the person for these chemicals and found that self-harming behaviour decreased significantly.

Appendix II
Further Reading

The following is by no means a comprehensive reference list. We have included books that focus specifically on self-harm or that have particular relevance to the issue.

Gloria Babiker and Lois Arnold, *The Language of Injury: Comprehending Self-Mutilation*, BPS Books, Leicester, 1997.
This book is aimed at professionals, but offers an excellent overview of the literature and a very compelling analysis of self-injury.

Both The Basement Project and Bristol Crisis Service for Women produce publications on aspects of their work. Addresses in the resource section.

Armando Favazza, *Bodies Under Siege*, Johns Hopkins University Press, Baltimore, 1987.
This is included because it is a classic text on self-harm. Favazza also gives a comprehensive cross-cultural overview of socially-sanctioned self-mutilation by describing practices from other countries and cultures.

Diane Harrison, *Vicious Circles: An Exploration of Women and Self-harm in Society*, Good Practices in Mental Health, London, 1995.
Diane Harrison has written this book based on her own experiences as a woman who self-harms. She uses other women's experiences as well as her own. The book is divided into eight sections examining both the wider context within which self-harm occurs and the personal struggle for survival.

Diane Harrison, and edited by Janet Gorman, *Understanding Self Harm*, Mind Publications, London, 1994. Available from MIND Mail Order, Granta House, 15–19 Broad Way, London E15 4BQ.
A 10-page leaflet with sections on what self-harm is; why people do it; differences between self-harm and suicide; its relationship with sexual abuse; finding help; issues for mental health workers, for family and friends; and resources.

HMSO *Suicide and Self Injury in Prison: A literature review*, Home Office Research Study No 115, HMSO: London, 1990.
Interesting, if only in its dry approach to the topic. However, the figures on the incidence and prevalence in prisons are very disturbing.

Marsha Linehan, *Cognitive Behavioural Treatment of Borderline Personality Disorder* and *Skills Training Manual for Treating Borderline Personality Disorder*, both Guilford, New York, 1993.
Linehan describes her work with women who self-harm. Michaela Swales and Barry Kiehn have written 'An Overview of Dialectical Behaviour Therapy in the Treatment of Borderline Personality Disorder', 1995, in the Internet-based electronic journal 'Psychiatry On-Line' http://www.cityscape.co.uk/users/ad88/psych.htm

The Mental Health Foundation also publishes material on self-harm. These include: MHF Briefing 1 *Suicide and Deliberate Self Harm* ISBN 0 901944 49 1 and *Working With People Who Self-Injure* ISBN 0953 1348 06. The latter includes nine training modules which include trainer's notes, participative exercises, handouts and overheads. The materials have been developed through the Bristol Crisis Service for Women. Available from The Mental Health Foundation, 37 Mortimer Street, London W1N 8JU.

Dusty Miller, *Women who Hurt Themselves: A Book of Hope and Understanding*, Basic Books, New York, 1994. Dusty Miller's book provides a detailed description of her theory regarding trauma re-enactment which she feels is at the root of self-harming behaviour. The second part of the book describes her own therapeutic model of work.

Louise Pembroke, *Self-Harm: Perspectives from Personal Experience*, Survivors Speak Out, London, 1994. As the title states this short book includes personal testimonies from both men and women who self-harm. Louise's own testimony is the longest but she provides the reader with a disturbing insight into the services provided to 'help' those who self-harm as well as some useful suggestions for family and professionals. Additional publications include: L. Pembroke, *Self Injury: Myths and Common Sense*, National Self Harm Network, London, 1996 and L. Pembroke and A. Smith, *Minimising the Damage from Self Harm*, National Self-Harm Network, London, 1996. Address for the National Self-Harm Network is in the Resources Section.

B.W. Walsh and P.M. Rosen, *Self Mutilation: Theory, Research and Treatment*, Guilford, New York, 1988.

This book gives a good overview of conventional ways of viewing and treating self-harming behaviour.

Managing Self-Harm: Conference Proceedings
The proceedings of a recent national conference on self-harm (March 1997) organised in conjunction with the Henderson Hospital have been published. They can be ordered from SHARM2 Conference Secretariat, Mole Conferences, 47 Tidy Street, Brighton BN1 4EL.

For those of you who have access to the Internet, you can search for information and contacts. A very comprehensive site can be found at http://crystal.palace.net/~llama/psych/injury.html. This includes a message board primarily for people who support someone who self-harms, a chat room, a reader survey and general information on self-harm. From the message board you can get directions to access a message board specifically for self-harmers themselves.

Appendix III
Resources

The following is by no means comprehensive. It includes a range of services and organisations who may be able to help you get the support you need. When contacting an organisation, be sure to check whether you will need to pay for the service they are offering; whether or not you will be offered a helper of the same gender and race as yourself (if that is what you want); how accessible the service is; and whether they have childcare facilities. You may also want to check what training the staff have to provide the service they are offering, and what their policy is on confidentiality.

Resources Specifically focusing on Self-Harm Issues

The Basement Project
Offers group work and workshops on self-harm. Also runs training and provides research information and publications.
Contact: Lois Arnold/Ann Magill, PO Box 5, Abergavenny NP7 5XW. Tel: 01873 856524.

Bewerley Croft Hostel
Provides a women-only area where services offered include emotional support as well as group and individual therapy; medical support from psychiatrists, CPNs and GPs; and advice about welfare and housing rights. Staff are very accepting of a woman's right to self-harm and are keen to address the problem rather than ignoring it. Women are encouraged to become independent, taking responsibility for their lives.
Contact: Bill Penson at Northcote Drive, Leeds LS11 6NJ. Tel: 0113 246 8741.

Bristol Crisis Service for Women
Run by volunteers for women in emotional need. As well as telephone support there are self-help groups and a range of publications. In particular they focus on helping women cope with their distress. British Crisis Service for Women are prepared to act as a contact point for groups throughout the United Kingdom that are resources for women who self-harm. They have an extensive list of such resources.
Contact: PO Box 654, Bristol BS99 1XH. Tel: 0117 925 1119.

Cavalcade Productions Produce three videos presented by D. Calof, J. Briere and D. Miller, entitled:
 Self Injury I: Genesis, Forms and Functions (46 mins)
 Self Injury II: Clinical Issues and Interventions (42 mins)
 Understanding Self Injury (30 mins)
These are American videos so you would need to check compatibility with your video equipment. Contact: Cavalcade Productions, P.O. Box 2480, Nevada City, CA 95959. Email address: cavpro@nccn.net

Child Abuse Survivors Network
Will support women who self-harm as a consequence of childhood sexual abuse.

Contact: PO Box 1, London N1 7SN. Tel: 0171 833 3737.

Dudley Priority Health NHS Trust
Working as a team with the Priority Trust and Dudley Social Services, the hospital offers a self-harm after-care service which includes evaluation and assessment, crisis counselling, follow-up services and education.
Contact: DSH Aftercare Service, Bushey Fields Hospital, Bushley Fields Road, Dudley DY1 2LZ. Tel: 01384 457373 ext 2946.

Eating Disorders Association
A national charity offering information and help to people with anorexia or bulimia nervosa. Their magazine sometimes includes related issues, of which self-harming is one. They also offer support to families and friends, as well as professionals involved in treating eating disorders.
Contact: EDA at Sackville Place, 44 Magdalen Street, Norwich NR3 1JU. Tel: 01603 619090; helpline 01603 621414 Mon–Fri 9 a.m. to 6.30 p.m.

Hope of People Everywhere
A self-harm support group run by people who self-harm for both males and females. New members are met initially by two other members of the group to ascertain whether the group would be beneficial to them. They aim to minimise self-harm and to support each other through periods of crisis.
Contact: 79 Buckingham Road, Brighton, East Sussex BN1 3RJ. Tel: 01273 749099 Fax: 01273 202877.

The Maudsley Crisis Recovery Unit
Offers an in-patient unit for people who persistently self-harm as well as an out-patient service for self-harmers and abuse survivors between the ages of 17 and 40. In-patient services include counselling, assessment of individual needs,

understanding and support as well as peer groups and rehabilitation. The unit encourages assertiveness and reduces self-blame. Out-patient services consist of individual hourly sessions which generally last for about six months.

For referrals contact: Dr M. J. Crowe, Consultant Psychiatrist, Maudsley Hospital, Denmark Hill, London SE5 8AZ. Tel: 0171 919 2371.

Mental Health Services for Children and Adolescents, Taunton

A young people's unit that specifically offers support to young people with eating disorders and self-harm. It offers 24-hour care, seven days a week.

Contact: Maria Symons, Unit Manager, Orchard Lodge Young People's Unit, Dene Road, Norton Fitzwarren, Taunton, Somerset TA4 1DB. Tel: 01823 432211.

Mental Health Foundation

21 Cornwall Terrace, London NW1 4QL. Tel: 0171 535 7400

The Mental Health Foundation has a number of publications and training resources on self-harming.

MINDlink

Although not specifically an organisation for women who self-harm, this is for mental health survivors, many of whom self-harm. MINDlink is a network of 1,400 survivors around England and Wales who influence MIND's policies and campaigning. It is a free service.

Contact: Madeline Chapman, MINDlink Coordinator, MIND, Granta House, 15–19 Broadway, Stratford, London E15 4BQ. Tel: London 0181 522 1728; Outside London 0345 660 163.

MIND Publications also offer a booklet entitled 'Understanding Self-Harm'.

Poole Group Therapy Unit
This unit offers a programme of individual and group therapy sessions on an out-patient basis. They see self-harm as part of the spectrum of issues raised by clients.
Contact: Christine Pearson, Consultant Clinical Psychologist, Herbert Hospital, Almhurst Road, Westbourne, Bournemouth, Dorset BH4 8EP. Tel: 01202 765323.

Scratch Videos A video about self-harm, *Visible Memories* by Richard Pacitti, can be obtained from: Scratch Videos, Cornerstone, 14 Willis Road, Croydon CR0 2XX. Tel: 0181 665 0210.

Shout
A bi-monthly newsletter offering support to women affected by self-harm. It includes not only people who self-harm but also groups and professionals who work with self-harm, and details of helplines, groups and resources.
Contact: PO Box 654, Bristol BS99 1XH.

Safe
A small charity which runs a national telephone helpline for people who have been ritually or satanically abused. Although not dealing specifically with self-harm, it will address the issue if it arises because of ritual or satanic abuse.
Contact: PO Box 1557, 106 Exeter Street, Salisbury, Wiltshire SP1 2TP. Tel: 01722 410889 Mon 6.30 – 8.30 p.m.; Tues 7 – 9.30 p.m.; Sat 10.30 a.m. – 12.30 p.m.

National Self-Harm Network
Campaigns for rights and understanding of self-harm. Publishes a guide for relatives and friends attending Accident & Emergency departments. Also available is a book entitled 'Self-harm perspectives from a personal experience'.

Contact: Louise Pembroke, PO Box 16190, London NW1 2WW.

Threshold

Aims to identify the mental health needs of women and to facilitate a realistic response to those needs. They offer prevention, support and resolution in complete safety.
Contact: 14 St Georges Place, London Road, Brighton, East Sussex BN1 4GB. Tel: 01273 622886.

Trust For the Study of Adolescence

Produces audio tapes and booklets on a wide range of topics including self-harm, aimed at teenagers, their parents and professionals who work with them.
Contact: Nadine Swift, Publications Manager, 23 New Road, Brighton, East Sussex BN1 1WZ. Tel: 01273 693311.

Women Against Rape

Although not specifically aimed at those who self-harm, WAR will deal with self-harming issues that arise for rape survivors. They offer counselling, support, legal advice, information and campaigning.
Contact: Crossroads Women's Centre, 230a Kentish Town Road, London NW5 2AB. Tel: 0171 482 2496.

Women Who Self-Harm Support Group

Meets on the first Saturday of each month. Call Quibilah for details.
Contact: Hulme Centre, off Chichester Road, Manchester M15. Tel: 0161 226 0787.

Additional Treatment Resources

Many alternative therapies have national bodies which disseminate information and register practitioners. It is always useful to contact these bodies when looking for someone to help you unless you have been given a recommendation by someone you trust. If you are unhappy about any treatment you receive you should complain through the national bodies.

Institute of Complementary Medicine
Contact: PO Box 194, London SE16 1QZ. Tel: 0171 237 5165.

British Acupuncture Council
Contact: Park House, 206–208 Latimer Road, London W10 6RE. Tel: 0181 964 0222.

The British Homeopathic Association
Contact: 27A Devonshire Street, London W1N 1RJ. Tel: 0171 935 2163

These are just a few of the possible alternative and complementary therapies. You might like to consider what is best for you.

General Counselling Resources

Afro-Caribbean Drop-in Group
Meets Wednesdays.
Contact: Our Chance Project, Thomas Street, St Agnes, Bristol. Tel: 0117 954 0505.

African-Caribbean Mental Health Association
Provides counselling and psychotherapy to all black people of African and Caribbean descent who have been through the mental heath system, and some who have not. Drop-in on Wednesdays or phone.
Contact: ACMHA, 35-37 Electric Avenue, Brixton, London SW9 8JP. Tel: 0171 737 3603.

British Association for Counselling
A national voice for counsellors, clients and supporters

of counselling. It offers a list of counsellors in every area as well as information and lists of publications.
Contact: BAC at 1 Regent Place, Rugby, Warwickshire CV21 2PJ. Tel: 01788 578328.

British Psychological Society
Produces a Directory of Clinical Psychologists annually. This provides information on Clinical Psychologists in your geographical area including their clinical specialisms. It should be available in your local library. If not the British Psychological Society can be contacted at: St Andrews House, 48 Princess Road East, Leicester LE7 7DR. Tel: 0116 254 9568.

International Association of Hypno-Analysts
Offers a register of practitioners which is available by writing or by telephoning.
Contact: PO Box 180, Bournemouth, Dorset BH3 7YR. Tel: 01202 316496.

PACE
Offers a counselling service for lesbian and gay men.
Contact: 34 Hartham Road, London N7 9JL. Tel: 0171 700 1323.

POPAN
Prevention of Professional Abuse Network.
Contact: 1 Wyvil Court, 10 Wyvill Road, London SW8 2TG. Tel: 0171 622 6334.

UKCP
UKCP is a national body which has lists of accredited psychotherapists.
Contact: 167–169 Great Portland Street, London W1N 5FB. Tel: 0171 436 3002.

Westminster Pastoral Foundation
Provides a counselling and therapy service charged on a sliding scale according to costs. This service is available in places other than London – contact below to find out if there is one in your area:
23 Kensington Square, London W8 5HN. Tel: 0171 937 6956.

The Women's Therapy Centre
Provides individual and group therapy to women over the age of 18; training and education for professionals; advice and information to both women and professionals about therapy. It aims to provide all of its services to all women, and has a policy of prioritising women who would not usually have access to therapy.
Contact: 6–9 Manor Gardens, London N7 6JS. Tel: 0171 263 6200.

All the information included in this resource file has been checked and updated, however if you do find anything that has changed, or would like to make comments and/or recommendations, please do contact us care of The Women's Press.

The Women's Press is Britain's leading women's publishing house. Established in 1978, we publish high-quality fiction and non-fiction from outstanding women writers worldwide. Our exciting and diverse list includes literary fiction, detective novels, biography and autobiography, health, women's studies, handbooks, literary criticism, psychology and self-help, the arts, our popular Livewire Books series for young women and the bestselling annual *Women Artists Diary* featuring beautiful colour and black-and-white illustrations from the best in contemporary women's art.

If you would like more information about our books or about our mail order book club, please send an A5 sae for our latest catalogue and complete list to:

The Sales Department
The Women's Press Ltd
34 Great Sutton Street
London EC1V 0DX
Tel: 0171 251 3007
Fax: 0171 608 1938

The Women's Press Handbook Series

Gerrilyn Smith and Kathy Nairne
Dealing with Depression

Second Edition – Fully revised and updated

Why do so many women suffer from depression? How can we defend ourselves against this common problem and get out of what can quickly become a vicious circle?

Gerrilyn Smith and Kathy Nairne, both clinical psychologists, draw on their extensive professional experience together with the experiences of a wide range of women sufferers to offer this down-to-earth and comprehensive guide to dealing with depression. Indentifying the many possible causes of depression, including bereavement and chronic illness, the authors also outline the many forms depression can take. Finally, they explore different ways of coping and recovering, and evaluate the help available, to offer an essential handbook for anyone who has experienced depression, either in themselves or others.

'A straightforward, practical guide . . . it explores its subject in depth.' *Company*

'I can thoroughly recommend this practical, sympathetic and non-patronising book.' *London Newspaper Group*

Health/Self-help £6.99
ISBN 0 7043 4443 2

Kay Douglas
Invisible Wounds
A Self-Help Guide for Women in Destructive Relationships

All couples have power struggles and disagreements at times, but
there is a difference between a relationship with the usual ups
and downs and one that constitutes emotional abuse. In this
practical and supportive book, Kay Douglas draws on the first
hand accounts of over 50 women – as well as her own personal
experience – to demonstrate how to recognise, resolve and
recover from a destructive relationship. With advice on how to
work out what is *really* happening within a relationship; how to
clarify needs and feelings; deal with an abusive partner; get the
support we need; cope with the effects on children; regain our
power in the relationship or decide to leave it; and how to heal,
this is an essential book for all women who have, or have had,
partners who are emotionally abusive.

Self-help £7.99
ISBN 0 7043 4450 5

The Women's Press Handbook Series

Gerrilyn Smith
The Protectors' Handbook
Reducing the Risk of Child Sexual Abuse
and Helping Children Recover

How much more effective would we be in working against child
sexual abuse if every adult had the knowledge currently available
only to professionals?

With child sexual abuse now unquestionably widespread, every
adult in contact with children must – and can – be an active
protector. Now, in this unique and essential book, child
psychologist Gerrilyn Smith gives adults all the information and
skills needed to protect children in their day-to-day lives. Drawing
on her many years of professional experience in the field, a wide
range of sources and proven techniques – as well as the
experiences of young survivors themselves – she offers a fully
comprehensive, practical and step-by-step guide to recognising,
reducing the risks, and overcoming the effects of abuse.

From being aware of the many possible signs of abuse to helping
a child confide, from creating the best context for recovery to
finding the most appropriate professional help, this urgently needed,
accessible book is absolutely essential reading for every adult.

Health/Self-help £6.99
ISBN 0 7043 4417 3

The Women's Press Handbook Series

Marilyn Lawrence
The Anorexic Experience

Third Edition – Fully revised and updated

Why does anorexia afflict so many women and girls? Why should a bright young woman suddenly drive herself to starvation?

Marilyn Lawrence, a professional with over ten years' specialist experience, offers a clear, accessible and helpful guide to recognising, understanding and tackling this insidious illness in yourself and others. From the fallacy of the 'ideal weight' to resolving the conflicts that can underpin an eating disorder, *The Anorexic Experience* also includes a complete review of the services and treatments currently available. Fully revised and updated, with vital new material, this invaluable handbook remains unmatched.

'An absorbing and important book.' *Nursing Times*

Health/Self-help £6.99
ISBN 0 7043 4441 6